PRAISE FOR

SEARCHING FOR NANNIE B.

Nancy Owen Nelson's memoir, *Searching for Nannie B.*, teaches us how to do family history and what we can learn from it. It is also a moving tale, simply told, of the everlasting connection between mothers and daughters. I wouldn't have missed it for the world.

Judith Hillman Paterson, author of *Sweet Mystery: A Southern Memoir of Family Alcoholism, Mental Illness, and Recovery*

Nancy Owen Nelson's memoir tells the story of three generations of amazing women whose lives are shaped, but not controlled, by early loss. Nelson's search for her grandmother's story touches the deep longing in all of us to discover who and whose we are. In the process, she discovers that the theological spectrum their life journeys span is shorter than she thought as she, Unitarian Universalist, is welcomed and embraced by the Primitive Baptist congregation where her grandmother worshiped.

My own adolescent years were enriched by friendship with Nancy and her Methodist mother. Her story evokes memories of early losses and the loving people who shaped my life. My hunch is it will do the same for other readers. .

The Rev. Paige Maxwell McRight, Doctor of Ministry, Presbyterian minister, Consultant to pastors and presbyteries and proud high school classmate of the author.

Nancy Owen Nelson's memoir, *Searching for Nannie B.*, is an engrossing story of three generations of women, starting from a grandmother who died giving birth to Nelson's mother, also named Nannie B. In fascinating detail we come to understand the women, their culture, their values, and the impact the loss of one of them had on the others.

Nahid Rachlin, author of *Persian Girls*

How do our lost ancestors touch us? Do they inform our consciousness? Nelson's voice of longing permeates this account of her search for a relative she never knew, a grandmother who died in childbirth. The mystery of why little is known about Nelson's maternal grandmother colors this highly readable exploration of self—a questioning of names, motives, and voices so close to Nelson's heart.

Elaine Greensmith Jordan, M.A.,M.Div. is the author of *Mrs. Ogg Played the Harp: Memories of Church and Love in the High Desert*

In Searching for Nannie B., readers follow a fascinating trail as Nancy Owen Nelson searches out the mystery of a gap in her own female linage, a grandmother who is never spoken of. The journey starts with her mother, the second Nannie B., then winds through real places and graves, through Ancestery.com, and through countless conversations as she tries to solve the enigma of the first Nannie B., her mother's mother. It is a trail that, at its end, cannot help but lead her to a better understanding of herself.

Susan Lang, author of the trilogy *Small Rocks Rising*

Searching for Nannie B.

Connecting Three Generations of Southern Women

Nancy Owen Nelson

The Ardent Writer Press
Brownsboro, Alabama

Visit Nancy Owen Nelson's Author Page
at

www.ArdentWriterPress.com

For general information about publishing with The Ardent Writer Press contact *steve@ardentwriterpress.com* or forward mail to: *The Ardent Writer Press, Box 25, Brownsboro, Alabama 35741.*

Cover by Jennifer Jones, Edmond, Oklahoma and The Ardent Writer Press. Composition and cover are covered by the same grant for noncommercial use noted above.

Cover photo of Nancy Owen Nelson by Joy Gaines-Friedler. Author page photos, graveyard photos, and that of the author and Priscilla Scott are provided by the author. Vintage family photos supplied by various family members, including Chris Hanlin, or the author. Photos supplied by government agencies credited on respective page.

ISBN 978-1-938667-37-4

Library of Congress Control Number: 2015906208
Library of Congress subject headings:
- BIOGRAPHY & AUTOBIOGRAPHY / Personal Memoirs.
- BIOGRAPHY & AUTOBIOGRAPHY / Women
- Autobiography--Personal narratives
- Autobiography--Miscellanea.

First Edition

ACKNOWLEDGEMENTS

MY JOURNEY TO "FIND" and understand my mysterious grandmother could have been a very lonely process. I have many people to thank for supporting me along the way. My writing group, Mary Assel, Joy Gaines-Friedler, and Alexander Morgan, accompanied me during the process as I wrote chapters, discovered both facts and truths, dipped into despair and rose to joy--to understand the meaning and purpose behind what I was doing. My dear friend, editor, and agent Kate Robinson gave invaluable support; she found a home for *Searching for Nannie B.* with Ardent Writers Press. I thank Springfed Arts and its director, John D. Lamb, for the opportunity to read from my book and to teach memoir workshops which feed my craft. M.L. Liebler has nurtured me and many other Detroit area writers and invited me to read from the manuscript. Reverend Roger Mohr of First Unitarian Universalist Church of Detroit, as well as the First UU congregation, gave both friendship and support to me during the process. Rev. Sherman Isbell shared his vast knowledge of the Primitive Baptist Church, which furthered my understanding of my family history and faith. Martha E. Jones, whose grandmother was best friends with mine, provided me with family contacts and history about the era in which Nannie B Russell Chandler lived. Priscilla Scott, New Hope genealogist, was invaluable—without her I would never have found my grandmother's grave. John Ed Butler, Bethel Cemetery proprietor, guided me through the Bethel Church graveyard, and the kind and loving folks of the Bethel Primitive Baptist Church welcomed me to join in their worship. My distant cousin, Dixie Leesnitzer, sent me the two buttons from my grandmother's clothes which her grandmother, now deceased Helen Robinson Paschal, had kept for decades. And before she passed, Helen provided me with stories about my grandmother passed down through the generations. My mother's last living sibling, David Chandler, asked questions and then lovingly understood. My sister Betty shared her family stories along with laughter and encouragement.

Numerous friends have cheered me on during this process. There are too many to name, but you know who you are. I thank Dr. Vicky Young for her support as reader and Dr. Michael F. Finn for his sage wisdom. I thank Jason Lucas for alerting me to the possibilities of Epinegetics. My Alabama friends have housed and encouraged me during my research. (You, too, know who you are). Finally, my husband, Roger D. Zeigler, has been there in body and spirit from the beginning.

Nancy Owen Nelson

Contents

FOREWORD

NANCY OWEN NELSON AND I are connected by the shared affirmation of our Unitarian Universalist religious tradition. Foundational to that tradition is a deep interest and affirmation of "the individual search for truth and meaning," about an understanding of the self as an evolutionary project. For our tradition, individuals are responsible for their own development and judgments and must be free to learn and grow, to create their own meaning and narrative. For Unitarian Universalists, living is an act of self-creation, of building a better and better person out of the raw materials of time and chance. We have both the opportunity and responsibility to become our best selves, to the best of our abilities and in our best understanding. For us, the search for truth and meaning is an act of religious devotion.

In that search for truth and meaning, it is often important to return to our families, as does Nelson in this memoir. The ancestral histories provide a wealth of clues about who and why we are ourselves. Within this process, we learn about those histories through our families' oral traditions. We hear the story of ourselves and our forebears as told by our parents, and perhaps our grandparents, aunts and uncles, siblings and cousins, and even family friends. This picture of our identities and ourselves is often formed on the basis of this tapestry of interwoven narratives and anecdotes. We begin to understand our roles within the larger ensemble because we can place ourselves relative to the other players, the other characters appearing in the larger fabric of the family.

The discovery of these stories does not always tell as much as we might like. Often the tapestry of family history does not seem to offer us the sort of clarity about who we have become, and why. And sometimes the narrative tells us a story about ourselves that we do not wish to accept. For those who experience this sort of longing for deeper clarity or direction in the story of himself or herself, we must step behind the tapestry, examine the back of the needlework, and reassess the images in our own terms—despite any risks to our understanding.

Nancy Owen Nelson's journey of discovery is exactly about this search for the truth and meaning in her own narrative that had been lost with her maternal grandmother. In finding those broken threads of her story, she creates a fuller and deeper sense of her own meaning and identity—as daughter, as mother, as woman, and simply as herself. Her process of rediscovering and reimagining the woman who gave birth to her mother, but who was lost in the larger family history, is also an opportunity for revisioning and redefining the personal narrative. In that sense, this book is as much about Nelson's development as a character in the story as it is about the process of discovering her grandmother's character and history.

The primary story presented here is about Nelson's travels and research to find out all she could about a grandmother she never met. That search was fruitful, and she is increasingly able to pull together threads of her grandmother's story and identity to flesh out her own image of herself, her mother, and her family. As she comes to understand her grandmother, the family tapestry begins to include her own story and lineage. Moreover, the places where the history had been somewhat threadbare become much more fully woven and coherent. In discovering her grandmother, she has very much enriched the story with greater truth, and greater meaning.

Yet this memoir also tells another story: it tells the story of Nelson reconnecting with the family and places her grandmother had known. She not only reconstructs the narrative for herself, but reintroduces her own character into the larger family narrative. She is no longer absent from the tapestry, nor is her mother, or her grandmother. They once again appear together as characters in the larger history. By her interactions with her mother's people and places, Nancy instantiates not just herself, although that is certainly part of the project, but she also speaks for all these women in her family line. She says to them, "We are here. We are part of this. Remember us." Because she reached out for information, she also reached out for relationship. For recognition. In seeking her grandmother, she offers herself and instantiates her entire lineage.

In closing this foreword, then, I commend this memoir to you as an act of self-creation as well as self-discovery. The work of researching family history is in one sense about learning about the past. In creating the narrative, we also are creating ourselves. But perhaps most importantly, as we reach out to gather the stories and details from which to weave the narrative, we also reach out to others, weaving new relationships and connections in the present, as well. May the scenes we add to the tapestry be a blessing to all.

The Reverend Roger Mohr, Doctor of Ministry
ABD Minister
First Unitarian Universalist Church of Detroit

DEDICATION

To My Grandmother
To My Mother

*Little Girl Nannie B. Chandler
with an unknown neighbor boy*

PREFACE

THE LITTLE GIRL IS TEN YEARS OLD. *She stands before her mother's grave in a cemetery near New Hope, Alabama. In my mind's eye, she is a small-framed little girl, with shoulders hunched, looking down at the headstone. The stone is crude, doesn't have much writing—just her mother's name, "Nanie B," misspelled, and "Wife of R. E. Chandler."*

The girl is trying to understand what happened, why her mother died. Two women walk nearby. She hears them talking.

"It's too bad the baby lived and Nannie B. died."

This statement echoes in my mother's memory for eighty-six years, the rest of her life. My mother will never get past this burden, this pain.

But she will hold onto her mother's name.
At least she has that.

Robert E. and Nannie B. Russell Chandler's daughter,
Nannie B. Chandler, at a few months old, with her father

CHAPTER ONE

Beginnings

"GOOD MORNING, NANNIE." The aide places my mother's breakfast on the table next to her bed. "How are *we* today?"

Nannie B. Nelson draws in a sharp breath. She grasps her bed rails with both hands, gnarled with arthritis, and tries to sit up and straighten her bent back.

She looks in the direction of the voice. All she can see is the outline of the aide's body. Macular degeneration has stolen the center of her vision.

"It's Nannie *B.*" She emphasizes the middle initial, her voice a mix of irritation and boldness. Then she adds. "It's my mother's name. She died an hour after I was born."

Throughout her life, my mother has defended her unusual name for what seems like a thousand times. She will do it as long as she must, in this nursing home, at the doctor's office, in the hospital where she goes for emergencies, in my home with my friends.

This will be her lifelong battle, to hold on to the precious name, one of the few things her mother left her. As if by saying it out loud, it brings her mother back to life. As if it recovers what was lost.

***

NANNIE B. CHANDLER NELSON knew very little about Nannie B. Russell, the woman who was her mother. When she was growing up, the only time when anyone ever spoke of her mother was the day Nannie B.'s father cried as he listened to her play the piano.

"You remind me of your mother when you play," he said in a voice choked with tears.

After his wife's death and his daughter's birth on July 12, 1905, my grandfather, Robert Edward Chandler, could not care for his baby girl alone. An aunt, Mary Russell Humphrey, who had daughters and a small boy, took in my mother. Then at about age three, Nannie B. met the woman who would be her stepmother, Nannie Dixie. Mom's father and stepmother would create a big family, with three boys and four girls.

Little Nannie B. was supposed to become a part of the family.

Instead, she often told me, she felt like an outsider, never fitting in, as if there was a shadow of shame she could not identify.

Around her mother's name were whispers, then silence. No one spoke it.

One Christmas in the 1960s my sister Marge surprised Mom with a photograph of Nannie B. Russell reproduced from a group picture of the four Russell sisters—Mary, Minerva, Sarah, and Nannie B. I remember that Mom cried when she opened the package. In the photo, Nannie B. Russell appears a proud and beautiful woman, her hair lifted into a Victorian twist and topped with a bow, her neck wrapped with a silky tie. Through the years, I would hear stories about her lovely voice and her musical ability. This was what she left to her infant daughter when she died. This, and a hole in my mother's life, in her heart and soul.

***

I WAS TWELVE YEARS OLD when I found out that my maternal grandmother died in childbirth.

"Nancy." We are alone in the living room of our apartment in Sault Ste. Marie, Michigan, in mid-afternoon. My mother's voice is subdued, as if she's afraid to speak, or as if she can't breathe. She draws my name out, both syllables. She has not lost her southern accent, despite our many moves outside the South.

"My mother died when I was born. Big Mama is not your real grandmother."

I don't understand this at all. I think about how Big Mama always hugs me to her fulsome chest, pounds me between my skinny shoulder blades when we arrive from our latest Army assignment. She leaves me almost gasping for breath afterward.

How could she not be my grandmother? My mother speaks again.

"*I have my mother's name, Nannie B. I never knew her. She died an hour after I was born. I heard only stories from some of her kin. I can tell you stories about her.*" My attention shifts. I'm anxious to leave this sad room, where my mother is telling me these sad things.

I don't want to know more right now. I just want things to be like they were before this afternoon, when Big Mama was my grandmother, when Mom wasn't telling me sad things.

I will not think very much about Nannie B. Russell until over fifty years later, after my mother has been dead for ten years.

***

THE MYSTERY OF MY GRANDMOTHER has haunted me since my mother's death in 2001. I want to know about Nannie B. Russell. I want to know why no one would speak of her, why no one helped the little Nannie B. Chandler understand that she was not responsible for her mother's death. I want to know why the only record I can find is the certificate issued by the State of Alabama, Madison County, for the marriage of R. E. Chandler to Nannie B. Russell, July 26, 1904. And why the State of Alabama agencies can find nothing else: no death certificate, no obituary, and no burial site.

Where is the cemetery where my mother stood more than 100 years ago? Is the gravestone covered with grass and weeds, dirt washed over it by heavy rains?

I want to find the grave, but I think that everyone who might know where it is must be dead.

19

The Marriage Certificate for Robert E. Chandler and Nannie B. Russell from 1904.

(Courtesy of the Madison County Records Center)

Most of all, I want to understand what this legacy of silence and guilt has meant for my mother, and for me.

For as long as I can remember, I've wanted to rescue my mother from invisibility, from having only the roots of her father's line, the Chandlers, which she will share with six siblings. I've wanted to rescue her from a feeling that she belonged nowhere.

I didn't realize that all along that I also felt as if *I* belonged nowhere.

In my own life as a military child, I always looked to the Alabama of my grandparents as my home. Papa and Mama Steve Nelson lived their whole lives there until their deaths in the early 1960s. Big Mama (Nannie Dixie) Chandler, my step-grandmother, died in the 1970s. My grandfather, Robert E. Chandler, died before I was born.

I seem to have inherited my mother's sense of not belonging. Maybe finding Nannie B. Russell's grave will answer some of my questions about belonging.

***

IN NOVEMBER OF 2011, I begin a search for my grandmother on Ancestry.com. I come across the Robinson line that connects to Nannie Dixie Robinson Chandler, my step-grandmother. On the Ancestry.com message system, I send a message to a man who is building the Robinson family tree. I ask him if he knows anything about Nannie B. Russell.

"Who told you about a Nannie B. Russell?" The tone of his return message is gruff, as if I've violated his privacy. Is he really asking, *How dare you find another wife for Robert E. Chandler?*

This feels like the same question that may have been asked for a century. *How dare Nannie B. Chandler have any mother other than Nannie Dixie, "Big Mama"?*

I answer him firmly. "My mother told me. She visited her mother's grave several times. I have a marriage certificate for Robert and Nannie B."

I lose sleep that night because of the tone on the man's email. *Why do people have trouble talking about my grandmother?*

It's as if her Nannie B.'s very existence is a blot on the Chandler history, on my mother's life, on the baby who caused her mother to die.

Don't talk about that other Nannie B. It's too shameful, or too sad. It could put a mark on the other Robert Chandler family, the one that remained intact for decades after Nannie B. Russell Chandler was put in the ground.

My next exchange with the Robinson relative is more positive. "Okay, then, I'll look at this. It's interesting."

He does find her later, as well as her parents, John R. Russell and Delilah Jane Chapman.

Now I can move forward. At least someone out in the world has acknowledged Nannie B. Russell.

***

I SPEND HOURS ON ANCESTRY.COM, and I do not realize the passing time. I never tire of the search. One Friday afternoon I even miss the first half of a union meeting because I am so caught up in this search.

I investigate my father's family—the Nelsons and Owens—back to a great, great grandfather, William Owen, who fought at Shiloh, was widowed at sixty-nine, and remarried at seventy. But I'm more drawn to my mother's family, to the mystery that is my Grandma Chandler. I trace Nannie B. Russell back two generations. Her parents, John R. Russell and Delilah Jane Chapman, had four girls. I wonder if Nannie B.'s father regretted not having any boys. I will later find out that an unnamed Russell infant boy is buried in the same graveyard as my grandmother and great grandparents.

I wonder too, where is the original photo of Nannie B. and her sisters?

I plan to travel to Alabama next summer. I will try to find Nannie B. Russell myself. I think if I do find her, somehow I will rectify the injustice of silence, shame, and emotional neglect that my mother suffered by not knowing anything about her.

***

CHRISTMAS EVE 2011. Roger and I decide to find a church service. We haven't located a church home since returning from Arizona in 2010. I find First Unitarian-Universalist Church of Detroit on the Internet. Their Christmas Eve carol service is at 7:00 p.m. We decide to attend.

The drive to downtown Detroit is only twenty minutes. On this cold, dark night in December, everything on I-94 is lit with Christmas lights—even some poorer houses and many businesses.

I haven't researched much about this church. When we arrive and park on Cass Avenue, we don't know which entrance to take. We end up going through an old mansion, down a long hall, and into a sanctuary lit by candlelight on all sides of the room. We are given small candles and a program of songs.

This church is very old, a neo-gothic architecture. I will later find out that it was built in 1916 and was a Universalist Church until it joined with the Unitarians in 1934 .

The air is filled with organ music. I am taken away as I look up at the chandeliers, the thirty-feet-tall organ pipes gleaming with a gold sheen in the candlelight.

The congregation sings carols and I feel the vibration of the huge pipe organ in my chest. I sing as I have not sung for a long time—open and unafraid.

I see Nannie B. Russell Chandler standing erect, her full-throated voice rising to sing Baptist hymns. I see my mother, Nannie B. Chandler Nelson, in front of me in the Methodist Church choir in Hartselle Alabama, singing the "Hallelujah Chorus" in full soprano while I harmonize in alto.

I must sing again. I must sing for my grandmother, and for my mother. I must give Nannie B. Russell a voice. Her voice was silenced much too soon.

A page from the 1928 Morgan County High School annual, Morcohi Volume IV, signed both with her maiden name and soon to be married name. Nannie B. Chandler Nelson taught only one year of school before being forced to retire. At that time, many school systems did not allow married women to teach.

CHAPTER TWO
By Many Names

BY MARRYING MY FATHER, Woodford Owen Nelson, and joining him in his military trek across the country, my mother set upon a path away from the college degree in Latin and French that she earned in 1927 at Howard College in Birmingham, Alabama (now Samford University).

After college, she taught only one year at Morgan County High School in North Alabama. During this year, she met my father and married him on March 16, 1928. At that time in the South, many school systems would not allow married women to teach. Nannie B. could finish the year out, and then she would have to resign. This bright young woman who taught English, French, and Latin, who sang with the chorus, would disappear from the school.

She would never hold a full-time job again.

My mother's teacher photo appears on a page near the back of the Morgan County High School annual, *Morcohi Volume IV, 1928*. She's sitting on a bench, ankles crossed, and her hands at rest on either side of her body. She's an attractive young woman, with bobbed hair, flapper-style, waved and parted on the right.

The caption under the photo reads, "MISS, OR MRS-?"

This is in the spring. By this time, she is most definitely *Mrs. Nelson*, no longer *Miss Chandler*.

In one of Mom's college Latin books, she writes her various signatures, sometimes diagonally, sometimes blocked, as if she is experimenting with who she really is.

Inside the school yearbook on the Ex Libris page, my mother signed her name two ways: "Nannie B. Chandler," letters slanted a bit to the right, and beneath it, "Mrs. W. O. Nelson," with the letters angled severely to the left. She ended this last signature with a period, as if she wanted to be definite.

My mother was no "Stoner," after Lucy Stone, nineteenth century abolitionist and suffragist who used her maiden name instead of her husband's. Nannie B. Chandler Nelson would follow the traditions of her time. She signed many versions of her married name: "Mrs. W. O. Nelson," "Mrs. Owen Nelson," "Mrs. Bee Nelson," "Mrs. Colonel W. O. Nelson," and "Mrs. Sergeant W. O. Nelson," after my dad's loss of rank following a bureaucratic error. On some covers of her sheet music, my mother often wrote two names, most often "Mrs. Owen Nelson" or "Mrs. W. O. Nelson." It was as if she couldn't decide which of her husband's names she preferred

Did she ever want to be Nannie B. Chandler again?

I suspect she did long for those days. She often said that the college years were some of her happiest. I can envision her playing vigorously for the men's glee club with the keyboard that had detached itself from its piano and perched on her knees. I can see her doing the Charleston, a dance she showed me many times, scooting across the floor with her knees moving toward and away from one another, toward and away. I can imagine her as the Maid of Honor in the court of Confederate General Lamkin, who, in the 1920s, survived to celebrate his Civil War exploits at the 32nd Annual Sons of Confederacy Veterans banquet.

This was all before she met and married a man who took her out of the Deep South and into a life of alternating excitement and despair, light and darkness. Never a pattern, never a predictable future.

CHAPTER THREE

Search

2012. Early in this new year, my search for Nannie B. Russell Chandler's grave drives my thoughts during the day and my dreams at night. When I'm not teaching or preparing for class, I spend every available moment researching. The search continues even in my sleep. I dream of driving a wagon with horses over muddy country roads. My mother is with me. All I know is that we are trying to find my grandmother's grave. I maneuver the horses away from the deep ruts, fearing we'll get mired in the mud. We come to a rushing stream and are unable to cross. It's too deep and fast.

The dream ends.

I continue my search on Ancestry.com, finding many Nannies and Nannys, but none matching my grandmother. It doesn't help my search that R. E. Chandler married another Nannie (middle name "Dixie") in 1908, three years after Nannie B.'s death.

My brain swirls with generations of Russells and Chapmans. One afternoon I type "Nannie B. Chandler" into the database for deaths in Alabama during the 1900s. Four entries down the list is a small window showing a portion of a typed document. The name "Nanie B Chandler" is highlighted.

I click on the window, and a document opens up: "Bethel Cemetery Records." "Nanie B, wife of R. E. Chandler."

No dates. Name misspelled.

My temples pulse. I think I've found her.

I search for Bethel Cemeteries and Primitive Baptist churches in Alabama. There is one Bethel Primitive Baptist Church in the northern part of the state—in Asbury, on Sand Mountain. I click on the link and find a long piece about the history of the cemetery, how during the Civil War the church members were against slavery and hid southern folks who sympathized with the Union.

How great would it be to find the legacy of social justice on my mother's side, the same values that my father had given my sisters and me! Dad taught us not to hate, to see the justice in the black people's march for civil rights.

At this point, I'm not sure how these ideas connect with Primitive Baptist theology on my mother's side. All I do know is that my great grandfather, John R. Russell, had listed two "hired hands" on the 1890 Census. They were white.

I hope the family did not own slaves.

My mother told me that her father, Robert Chandler, was a strict Primitive Baptist. Also known as "Hard Shell Baptists," Primitive Baptists believe they are the chosen ones. They are predestined to salvation.

As I study the Asbury Church web site, I am reminded of a story about the time Mom and her sister, Norma, went forward to the altar to be saved during a revival. Before they arrived at the altar, their father caught up with them and pulled them out of the church.

"You may be going to hell, but you're going to bed first!" he told them as he led them out of the revival tent.

When I heard this story, I sensed that Mom thought her father was angry that night. Perhaps little Nannie B. mistook his reaction for conviction, But when I would meet Primitive Baptists later in this search, I would not be confronted by the notion of hellfire and damnation. I would be treated with kindness. Indeed, I would later read in the history of the New Hope Primitive Baptist Church my ancestors attended that "the man who wants salvation, fears God and loves God, is the subject of grace."[i]

I begin to research the Primitive Baptist faith. I remember the fundamentalist revivals of my youth at the Hartselle, Alabama campgrounds and thought it might be useful to explore my revival site as well. During my Methodist Church days in high school, everyone would attend the "Tabernacle," an outdoor sanctuary with dormitories and a kitchen, for longer events. It was a religious campground since 1899.

When I check the website for the Tabernacle, I see that it has not changed its schedule for decades. It runs during the summer, from Friday to Friday, with three worship sessions a day. I observe that all of the ministers listed are from even stricter theologies than my "in town" Methodist Church. Very seldom at the majestic, brown brick First United Methodist Church in Hartselle (built by a committee on which my paternal grandfather, Stephen Mae Nelson, served) would we be asked to declare our faith and salvation by going forward to the altar, as my mother and aunt had done so many years before. If the preachers asked us to come forward, rarely did they do it with raised voice, shouting about fire and brimstone and evil souls, fists punching the air. Yet, when I attended the Tabernacle as a guilty teenager, I felt the need to walk down. After all, I was stained, wasn't I? I didn't pray enough, I thought, and sometimes I wanted to avoid my church, my town, where everyone seemed so holy.

I wanted excitement, not guilt.

Many of my friends rushed to attend a revival with Billy Graham when he appeared near our town.

I didn't want Billy Graham; I wanted a boyfriend.

This religion felt like an ever-threatening net of conformity that I wanted to shrug off of my shoulders. Is the Primitive Baptist faith like this?

I email Reverend Sherman Isbell, the contact person for the Asbury Bethel Church. He is writing a book about the church and its community. He emails me that the Primitive Baptists came to the United States from England in the early to mid-nineteenth century. They separated from Missionary Baptists due to their Calvinist belief in predestined salvation. He writes that "The Primitive Baptists, as a movement arose in the American South in the period of the 1820s-1840s. There were Baptists who earlier came to America from England." He says further that for Primitive Baptists, revivals were "an outpouring of the Holy Spirit at divine initiative."[ii]

He asks to see the documents I have on my grandmother. I send him the 1900 U. S. Census that shows the John R. Russell family living in Poplar Ridge.

I'm so excited to find this Bethel church that I don't think about *where* Robert and Nannie B. lived. I should have realized that they never would have been listed on a census as a married couple, since they married in 1904 and she died in 1905—the census is taken every ten years at the beginning of a decade. The only thing I do know is that the Russell family lived in Poplar Ridge, near Gurley, Alabama.

Reverend Isbell writes back that my grandparents probably did not belong to the Asbury Bethel Church because Poplar Ridge is on the other side of what is now Lake Guntersville. It's about forty miles away from Sand Mountain. "At the beginning of the twentieth century the roads would have been difficult."[iii]

I have a mental image of my grandparents traveling on dirt roads after a rain. It is early 1905, and Nannie B. is a few months pregnant. Her husband Robert eases the horses over the bumps, holding the reins with his right hand while he rests his left hand gently on her belly.

In a few months, she will be dead.

Nancy Owen Nelson

*The author (left) and genealogist Priscilla Scott
of New Hope, Alabama (right)*

CHAPTER FOUR

Finding the Grave

AFTER I FIND OUT that Nannie B. Russell Chandler could not have been buried in the Asbury Cemetery, I begin a Google map search for another Bethel Church about forty miles away. I locate one near the intersection of Cherry Tree and Poplar Ridge Roads. The site is a tiny mark on the map and shows a church and graveyard. An Internet search does not reveal a church office or contact information. I call the library in nearby Mount Hope.

"There's a local woman, Priscilla Scott, who is a genealogist and might be able to help you," the reference librarian tells me. She also says that Priscilla should be getting home about this time from her city genealogical committee meeting.

Where else but in a small town would people know one another's schedules?

I call Priscilla, gripping the phone tightly in my hand. *This cemetery could be where my grandmother is buried.*

After we talk for a moment about the cemetery, she agrees to look for Nannie B. Russell Chandler's grave.

Priscilla's accent has a southern flavor, with soft edges around the words. Somehow, I'm comforted by her voice, the language of my people, of my grandmother.

She will call me back.

I wait several days, and finally call her.

Searching for Nannie B.

"I found it," she says casually, as if she's found her lost keys or a hairpin. She's also found several Russell graves in the Yard Ten. Nearby is a grave that may be it. She tells me she will email me two photos, a map of the yard, and a list of those buried there.

A few minutes later, I open an e-mail with four attachments. The file is named "Scanned Russell Chandler."

Priscilla explains in her email that she took two photos, one full shot of Nannie B.'s gravestone with her mother's, Delilah Jane Chapman Russell's, back and to the side.

I open this one first, unable to wait any longer.

It's beautiful. Old, as if it hasn't been touched in decades. Graves behind it are decked with Confederate flags.

It's rested there for more than its century.

> *Moss—grown over*
> *stalwart stone*
> *Letters worn*
> *Corrugated like marble.*
> *106 years ago*
> *you were buried*
> *Below.*

I sit with the photo awhile, studying its detail. I am crying, for Nannie B., for my mother, for myself. I'm joyful and sad at the same time. I'm also angry.

> *Has anyone visited*
> *since your daughter,*
> *A ten-year-old, wondering*
> *Why her mother died?*
> *She lived a life*
> *Shaped by absence,*
> *A relic*
> *longed for.*

I think of the little girl who stood by her mother's grave, who heard the women speak about her as if she were a mistake, a horrible error of nature that took her mother away. I think of how, as my mother told me often, she felt the unspoken shame that would not allow her to fit into her new family. How many times afterward she would half-whisper to me, in moments of reflection, about her mother, what she was like, how musical she was. All of the things my mother would never know except second-hand, through stories from Russell kin later in her life.

I will go to Alabama in June. I will attend the Asbury Church reunion and talk to the people. I will visit the Poplar Ridge Bethel Cemetery and sit with my grandmother's grave, feel the energy of the Russells and Chapmans. I will look out over the fields that lie beyond the graveyard and imagine how it must have been in 1904, when Robert and Nannie B. married and began a life together. How it must have been in 1915, when my mother stood before her mother's grave, confused, sad, and lost.

Perhaps I can go inside the Bethel Church, sit in the pew where my grandmother sat, back straight, hair in a twist, fanning herself in the sultry Alabama heat while she sang with full-throated voice the hymns of salvation.

(Photos courtesy of City of Huntsville Geographic Information Sys Dept.)

***Nannie B. Russell attended this school
along with her best friend, Lucy Emma Butler.***

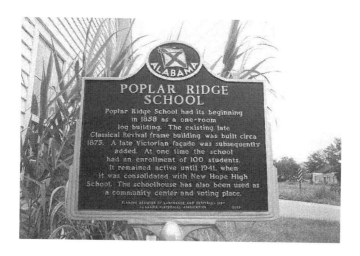

CHAPTER FIVE

The Herefords

FROM AS EARLY AS I CAN REMEMBER, Charlie and Rachel (Hereford) Oden lived next door to my Nelson grandparents, Steve and Ellie, or "Papa Steve" and "Mama Steve," as we called them. Rachel and Charlie were my parents' ages and had two daughters, Martha and Betty, and a son, Charlie.

For all those years until my grandparents passed in the early 1960s, Rachel and Charlie were there to help in any emergency.

I don't recall one occasion in particular. I only know that if anyone in the household called for Charlie, he would stride next door to the Nelsons', his long legs taking huge steps. He would be there in minutes after a phone call.

It was much later that I really *heard* what my mother had told me for years about Rachel, that she was a Hereford from Gurley, Alabama, and that her family knew my grandmother, Nannie B. Russell.

So many times, Mom and one of her half-sisters or a friend (probably Rachel) would drive to Gurley in Madison County, Alabama. Poplar Ridge was a community near Gurley where Nannie B. Russell and her family lived before marrying Robert Chandler in 1904. I know this only because Nannie B. is mentioned in her father's census in 1900. She is buried in Poplar Ridge, so they must have lived nearby, or perhaps in Gurley, which Mom mentioned often when talking about her mother. Once in my teens I went along with my mother for the ride through Mooresville, a historical town which is preserved in the manner of the nineteenth century. As we drove up one shaded street and down another, I remember that Mom said these houses were like the one her parents lived in. How did she know this? Who told her?

Where is Poplar Ridge? Is it anything like Mooresville? I can't even find the town on the map, only some signs that show the community once existed, such as Poplar Ridge Road, near the Old Bethel Cemetery. Some maps say it was a part of New Hope, while others say Gurley.

My memory of this trip is opaque, like watching a scene through filmy glass, or through cataracts. I remember the narrow, unpaved streets, the shapes of houses that seemed very old to my younger self. I remember no other details.

I ask myself why I didn't listen more. Why didn't I care?

At the time, the trips felt obligatory, as if I should be listening to my mother about her grief, as if I should have cared about it.

I tell myself it's the stuff of youth, the mind of a teen who goes along on the ride to Madison County out of a sense of duty. At that time, my mother seemed old-fashioned to me. I dismissed much of what she said as uninteresting.

Mom was almost a generation older than my friends' mothers. Having a baby at forty years old was rare in the mid-twentieth century. She told me that both of my grandmothers feared I'd be a mongoloid (now officially called Down's Syndrome) because of the "dangers" of an older woman delivering a baby.

Most likely when she had me, Mom also thought about her mother's death from childbirth.

***

RACHEL HEREFORD ODEN'S MOTHER, Lucy Emma Hereford Butler, was Nannie B. Russell's best friend. Rachel told Mom, and later told me, the stories she heard from her mother about Nannie B.—how they would stay overnight together, how they would spend hours on a porch swing, laughing and whispering, and how they attended the Poplar Ridge Community School together. They wrote what Rachel called "love letters" to one another, I imagine the sort of letters in the Victorian novels I've studied and taught. It was acceptable at the time that women could love one another in a particular way, as special friends. I've even read that the language is "ardent," [iv] which could suggest a love affair between lesbians. But such language could also signal the high importance of women's heterosexual friendships in that era.

Rachel gave me a vision of my grandmother's dignity and graceful demeanor in church, about how beautifully she sang, how she held herself proudly erect at the Old Bethel Primitive Baptist Church.

Like my trips to Madison County and my mother's tales of her separateness from the family, I never listened closely to all these stories until 2002, the last time I saw Rachel in an assisted living home. That day I finally realized that I needed to find out more. I took notes.

***

NOW THAT I AM in the midst of ancestral research, I open the journal where I put the notes of that trip through Alabama:

May 24, 2002. Rachel talks in her usual fast clip, running her words together. *Your mama's mama was a beautiful woman. My grandmother Lucy loved her… wrote love letters to each other. Nannie B. would sit and fan herself in church. She was lovely.*

She also talks about Mom. *People would stand in line to help your mother.*

Rachel is right. I never understood why, but my mother was able to charm almost anyone, not with the false sweetness of a Southern belle, but with a genuine interest in people. As my son Owen said recently, "Mama Bee would treat Attila the Hun with kindness."

What would her mother Nannie B. Russell have been like if she'd lived longer?

I recall the many boyfriends I had after leaving home, how I would tell Mom about them on the phone; and when they visited, how she always treated them graciously. Even Kip, my ex-Hell's Angels lover, who looked like he still belonged with the Angels—his long hair and beard, mustache, his muscled arms. He was a musician, sang music of the Allman Brothers.

Mom and Kip took to each other immediately. Before I knew it, he was strumming his guitar while Mom found the tune on her piano.

I decide to research the Hereford line. I begin a family tree on Ancestry.com. I want to call Rachel's and Charlie's daughter, Martha Emma.

For a day or two, I research her on the Internet, unable to get an address or phone number. Finally, I look at my journal notes from my visit with Rachel almost ten years before. I find Martha's phone numbers listed at the bottom of the page where I wrote Rachel's comments.

I chastise myself for not looking sooner.

When I call Martha Emma, we chat for a few minutes, realizing it's been almost forty years since we saw one another, in the 1970s at Auburn University. I was in graduate school pursuing my Master's degree in English.

It feels like yesterday.

Martha speaks quickly, like her mother. She says she's at the end of her life. I'm two years older than she is. What is she talking about?

"Martha, you'll live a long time. So will I," I tell her.

Martha goes on about "funeralizing" her house, as her mother Rachel said often in her later years. Months later, Martha will tell me on another phone call that after Nannie B's best friend died, Martha's grandmother Lucy, Rachel built a bonfire, opened a second floor window, and threw most of Lucy's papers in the fire. Destroyed, any evidence of important friendship between Lucy and Nannie B. Lost, most likely, any first-hand evidence of my grandmother, letters which she may have crafted with ink and flowery stationary. I want to see these pages, hold them in my hands.

How could Rachel "funeralize" Lucy's papers without going through them? Obviously many folks are not like I am—an archivist of family records, sometimes to a fault, when the old clippings and notes and photos have begun to decay in the scrapbooks and boxes which contain them.

And how can Martha Emma talk about death when I'm just starting to search for my grandmother? I plan to live as long as my mother. Maybe ninety-six years won't be so old by that time.

And maybe I'll figure out what happened to Nannie B. Russell, why she "disappeared" from family lore or conversation when she died.

Our conversation continues and Martha offers to send me a list of her family members, with contact information. She will also send a chapter in a book about the Herefords. It's about Lucy.

When I receive the package, I read over the little chapter about "Lucy Emma Butler Hereford (1878)" [v] several times, hoping to gain some glimpse, any hint, of my grandmother. I also research the Poplar Ridge Community School that Nannie B. and Lucy attended. Poplar Ridge is now on the National Registry of Landmarks and Heritage. The one-room schoolhouse built in 1858 was reconstructed into a Victorian frame in 1875, over two decades before Nannie B. Russell was born. She and Lucy, along with other children from the community (up to one hundred, according to historical records) attended this simple wood frame building for who knows how long? The chapter on Lucy says she went through "the highest grade offered at the time" and then to boarding school for six years in Tennessee, at State Normal School. She received her A. B. at the end of those six years, which suggests to me that Poplar Ridge went through the tenth grade, leaving the last two grades for transfer, if the student's parents chose to send her.

Did Nannie B. also go on for more schooling? I can't imagine my grandmother not continuing school. Perhaps I think this because my mother finished her B.A. in French, Latin, and English. Surely

41

her mother, Nannie B., studied the classics. Education at that time was a strict regimen of reading, writing and math, sprinkled with moral training and communal chores. Elocution, the Pledge of Allegiance, the Lord's Prayer, spelling lessons, and chores at the end of the week to clean up the school. School was bare bones and pragmatic. Even as late as the 1920s, as author and poet Jesse Stuart relates in his memoir, *The Thread that Runs So True*, he began to teach in a one-room schoolhouse in the rugged hills of Kentucky. For him, life was challenging at best, as the children often came from very poor families. One teacher taught all of the grades.

Perhaps my grandmother pursued her interest in music. The chapter on Lucy says that after graduation from State Normal, she returned home to teach piano lessons in her home. I'm sure her best friend, Nannie B. Russell, also visited Lucy's home and sang while she played. Or perhaps Nannie B. played with her, a duet, perhaps Beethoven's *Minuet in G*. More likely, they played hymns from a Primitive Baptist hymnal.

I'll probably never know the answers to these questions. The letters, diaries or journal written by Nannie B. or Lucy were burned. But I can hope. There's always the chance that someone kept some of Lucy's correspondence.

After taking a teaching job for one year in Delrose, Tennessee, Lucy Emma Butler married the principal of the school, Josiah McCracken Hereford, in 1901. What is not said is that Lucy, the "school marm," was probably not encouraged to teach after marriage. As with my mother twenty years later, Lucy served one year as a professional. Her all-important job was not to teach others' children, but to attend to her husband and her own children. Lucy had fourteen.

And where is my grandmother in all of this? I'm disappointed that Nannie B. Russell remains invisible in this little account.

I would have thought as Lucy's best friend, she would be her maid of honor in her wedding. Not so. Another young woman, Victoria Butler, stood with her at her marriage vows. With the name "Butler," I imagine Victoria was a relative, a cousin perhaps.

There's no sign of my grandmother in the chapter. Did she even attend the wedding? In 1901, she would have been twenty-two years old and not yet married. Did she long for a lovely wedding for herself, with the "wedding dinner feast" provided for Lucy and Josiah?

I'm seeing a pattern in the lives of southern women during the turn of and early twentieth century. For these women from families of some means (though certainly not rich), college was a possibility. Again, I wonder if my grandmother attended school after she left Poplar Ridge. Or did she marry with plans to be a wife and mother?

For such a short time.

***

DAYS PASS AND I CONTINUE my research of the Hereford family. Martha Emma has sent me a full list of the family back to Lucy Hereford Butler's parents. Some of Lucy's children are still living. Martha suggests I call the two brothers, Billy and Bledsoe. The youngest son, Bledsoe, lived with his mother until she passed when he was fifty years old. Maybe Billy will know something. Maybe he'll remember his mother talking about Nannie B., or maybe he will have letters or journals.

But first, I call the man who is connected to my great-grandparents' church, Bethel Primitive Baptist. John Ed Butler answers the phone after several rings. I recognize the deep accent of Alabama hill people.

"Hello, Mr. Butler. I'm Nancy Owen Nelson, a family friend of the Herefords. My grandmother is buried in the Old Bethel Cemetery."

I speak louder than usual, expecting that John Ed may have trouble hearing. I tell him that I plan a trip in June to visit the church and cemetery.

He says he'll be happy to see me and show me the church. I can attend a service if I want to.

"The church had a fire. They tore the old one down and built another one. I kept one of the pews and put half of it in my house."

I'm disappointed that I won't be able to see the church where Nannie B. Russell actually sat, where she fanned herself, where she stood to sing.

But I want the other half of the pew! I wonder if it's still intact. I don't ask, but I do begin to imagine getting a half of a strong cedar pew, carved by hands of nineteenth century craftsmen, into the back of my Ford Escape.

It could be the very pew where Nannie B. sat.

Running through my mind is the possibility that her DNA is still on that pew. I remember that after my mother died, I sat on the floor in our guest room going through her personal things. There was a brush with her hair still in it. I combed through it and put the hair in a small plastic bag. Tears coursed down my cheeks and onto the carpet. I missed my mother so much that my chest ached. I imagined cloning her. I had plenty of DNA in that clump of hair.

And now, the thought of getting even closer to the essence of my grandmother by visiting her church excites me.

Maybe the pew would still be there. Maybe I could take it home.

***

AFTER HANGING UP from my conversation with John Ed Butler, I write him a letter. I make sure to thank him first for talking with me, and I show my happiness at finding my grandmother's grave. Then I reinforce what I've said on the phone—that I want to visit him and the church, to see the pew, and to look at any archives or records of the church. He has agreed on the phone to check beforehand with those church members who have the archives.

I tell him, too, that my sister Betty and I have decided to add another stone to our grandmother's grave. A stone to complete Nannie B. Russell Chandler's years, to commemorate the value she must have had to her husband, and the deep loss Robert Chandler must have felt.

Nancy Owen Nelson

Nannie B. Russell's Original Gravestone
(Note the headless lamb at top of the marker
and the misspelling of Nannie B. to Nanie B.,
later corrected by the author with a second marker)

CHAPTER SIX

Visiting the Grave

JUNE 5, 2012. I'm driving alone to Alabama to see my grandmother's grave. This first day on the road takes me to Louisville, Kentucky, where I spend the night in a motel. My second day's destination is Paducah, where my friend Janice and I will spend two days together. Madeleine, the third party of the "Gleesome Threesome" from my graduate school years, will join us.

For two days, we catch up on each other's lives, sharing memories and hysterical laughter about a crazier period when we often drank beer at the local pub, Peeps, even on nights when we had to teach or attend class the next day. We talk about our lives, Madeleine marrying and divorcing several times, and Janice marrying the first time at almost fifty years old. Janice seems happy after twenty years with Bob. I tell them that I've found my life partner in Roger.

As I narrate my marital stories, I think about how time, on the one hand, can seem static and unmoving, and on the other, gallop steadily forward, like the coach horse in Emily Dickinson's poem.

> *Because I could not stop for death,*
> *He kindly stopped for me.*
> *The carriage held but just ourselves*
> *And Immortality.*

Searching for Nannie B.

The subject of old age and illness arises often in our talk, and we discuss our physical health. As I listen to my friends talk, I realize what they've both faced over the last years of their lives—physical challenges, even brushes with death. I have not faced such issues.

Yet.

Perhaps I will. Their fortitude gives me hope for my own.

On the second day after my arrival, the three of us walk along the sidewalk next to the Ohio River, where a historical marker tells me Grant landed to occupy the City of Paducah in 1861. The day is beautiful, a pleasant seventy-five degrees. Children run in circles around their parents, and a couple snuggles against one another on a park bench. This is the slow-paced, southern scene of play and love.

My left foot hits an uneven patch of the sidewalk. My ankle twists, and I go down on the pavement, scraping my left knee and the palm of my right hand. Everyone but me is worried. I get up, brush off the dirt, dab a tissue on the small amount of blood on my hand and knee, and move forward.

"Maybe you're too old for those high sandals," one of my friends says. I start to defend my sandals and my ability to wear them safely.

Then she says, "Just kidding."

I do hope she is kidding because I'm not ready to be "old" yet. I will fight the progression to old age as long as I can. I may not defy it, but I'll do my best to stave it off with my three-times-a-week yoga classes, my supplements and natural hormones.

Perhaps it is this search for Nannie B. Russell Chandler, for the truth of her shortened life and its impact on my mother's. Perhaps this is why I rail against aging.

I want to be alive and vital long enough to see Nannie B. Russell Chandler live again.

On my way to Alabama the next morning, I drive back east through Kentucky and pick up I-65, the highway that will lead me "home" to Hartselle, Alabama, and to the Hartselle City Cemetery, where my parents, aunts and uncles, grandparents and great grandparents on the Nelson side are buried. My great-grandmother,

Nancy Jane Thomason Owen, is buried next to her husband, Robert Goodman Owen. I am her namesake. Robert Owen died in front of a train in October 1929. I only happened on this startling information recently from a post on Ancestry.com. I made a note to find out more about that later.

I go to the Hartselle Cemetery first. I haven't seen my parents' graves since 2003, when Roger and I were on the way to visit Arizona before we moved out West. Despite the mowing by the cemetery staff, the grass has begun to encroach on these two low stones. My father's copper-toned, military stone is tarnished with dirt. My mother's, a deeper metallic color, also needs washing and cleaning. The two lines of her poem to my father barely show through the dirt:

"Reflections"

Eventide will come at last,
But our love will never die.

Tomorrow I will buy a brush and clippers. When I return to the graveyard, I will cut back the grass and scrub the dirt from the stones.

I arrive at my motel in time to shower, then drive to the nearby city of Decatur for dinner with friends.

Tomorrow morning. After seeing to my parents' graves, I will head for New Hope, Alabama, a town near the graveyard where my Grandmother Chandler is buried.

***

SATURDAY, JUNE 9. New Hope, Alabama is only twenty miles from Huntsville, a thriving city as a result of NASA's Marshall Space Flight Center and Redstone Arsenal. I decide to drive around the city of Huntsville this time. Instead, I take the back roads to New Hope, through the green-clad hills at the edge of the Appalachian Mountains. The northern border of Madison County, where New Hope resides, brushes up against the Tennessee state line.

Searching for Nannie B.

As I drive the curving, two-lane roads, I listen to Celtic music. *This must be the music of the Scots-Irish, the people who settled this area. This must be the music my ancestors heard in their community gatherings.*

The road curves and slopes. I pass only a few cars. I am embraced by a rich, green shelter. I am alone but I feel comforted.

I mind the speed limit. I want to arrive safely. This trip is too important for anything bad to happen.

In an hour, I enter the town, greeted by signs "Welcome to New Hope." The town is so small, in fact, that there appears to be only one street that could be called "downtown." At this point, my GPS loses the signal.

The day before, I had made plans to meet Priscilla Scott, the local genealogist, and John Ed Butler, the cemetery proprietor and cousin of Nannie B. Russell's friend, Lucy Butler, at John Ed's house around 3:00 p.m. Now without the help of my GPS, I'm unable to find John Ed's house. I stop the car and take a deep breath, trying to calm myself. I will call Priscilla.

I reach her on the phone and she directs me to the library, which is only two blocks from where I am. I drive by a small business section, which I've passed a couple of times before, circling round and round the center of the town. When I arrive, I think I've come to the wrong place. The library is just a little store front, the size of a clothing store in any small town. Over the library is a banner that reads "Elizabeth Carpenter Public Library of New Hope." I greet Priscilla at the desk in the center of the room. She is unlike how I imagined her; she's a tall woman with short grey hair. I thought she would be dumpy, more grandmotherly-looking. As I watch her stand up to greet me, it's obvious that she, too, refuses to make a date with Dickenson's carriage driver. She moves toward me without hesitation, with a long stride.

As we talk, I can tell that Priscilla loves her work helping others with their family roots. I think it must keep her going. She lights up when she speaks of Nannie B.'s grave and the other families surrounding her in the Bethel Cemetery. In our conversations, she tells me she's "addicted" to people's family histories.

I understand that condition. I've been addicted since I began my search for my grandmother.

In the library, I buy a book on the Poplar Ridge School, where Nannie B. and Lucy Butler attended. I sit down to flip through the pages. But I'm impatient for 3:00 to arrive, when Priscilla will leave the library and lead me to John Ed's house on Cherry Tree Road, just up the road from the cemetery.

We leave a few minutes after 3:00. When we finally arrive at John Ed's house on Cherry Tree Road, he gets into my car and we follow Priscilla to the Bethel Cemetery, around more curves and past the Poplar Ridge Community School. I make a note to return to the school later.

I'm anxious to get to Nannie B. Russell.

Soon we turn left off of Cherry Tree Road onto Poplar Ridge Road, an even smaller road than the others I've taken to get here. Just after the turn, a field of tall corn stands in the sunlight. There are no other cars or trucks.

We park our cars, and Priscilla unlatches a metal fence. I wonder briefly why the cemetery isn't more protected. How easy it is to walk through the rusting gate and onto the grounds. Are the graves protected against … What? People ransacking the stones, breaking monuments? This feels like too holy a place for such behavior. I brush the thought away.

It's so very still here; the only occasional sounds are distant cars or trucks, and cicadas and doves in the trees nearby. There's a faint scent of mown grass.

I walk past family plots with large stones—Moon, Butler, Cooper, McPeters. I follow Priscilla to the left down a little hill, walking into a small sunken area that borders this side of the cemetery.

I see the gravestone, so much smaller that it seemed in the photo Priscilla sent me.

Searching for Nannie B.

Nanie B.
Wife of R. E. Chandler

I'm struck again by its almost primitive quality. By the lack of a message—no "beloved wife of," or "beloved mother." No dates. The first name is spelled incorrectly. A concrete lamb lies on the top of the stone, its head missing.

I feel anger and sorrow that she's been neglected so long.

I stand near the stone in the brown sundress I've worn for this special occasion. Priscilla takes my picture three times. For the first two shots, I do not smile. For the third, I do.

"It's always better to smile for these pictures," Priscilla says, breaking the quiet.

As Priscilla and John Ed walk about in the cemetery, I brush my hand over the lamb's neck, sharp, jagged concrete where the head was. I look around, imagining that I can spot the head of the lamb, but I see no broken concrete nearby, not even in the edge of the woods bordering the graveyard.

I imagine my ten-year-old mother standing in the little sunken area in front of her mother's gravestone, her hands folded. Her eyes are on the stone, and then she looks down to the ground, then again to the stone, as if imagining somehow that she could see her mother.

Standing alone with my grandmother's grave in this place of quiet, I feel the vibrations of history, the waves of grief and loss that must have rushed over Robert Chandler as he watched his young bride of less than a year die bearing his child. I think that perhaps he was too grief-stricken to make sure Nannie B. Russell Chandler had a proper stone to show her importance in his life, and in the life of the daughter who would never know her.

I also feel a gripping sadness in my chest, wishing my mother's sadness and loss eased, wishing to change the life she lived outside the comfort zone of family. I wish to relieve the guilt that she felt for a death she caused, but without ill will or foreknowledge.

All I can do is to bring Nannie B. Russell Chandler to life so that the world will know she existed, that she lived and loved her husband and the child she would not nurture. There is some consolation in that.

I must also try to understand why this journey to find my grandmother has such a grip on my life now, why I am obsessed with the task of discovery. What am I searching for?

While in the graveyard, I take pictures of the other Russell gravestones, Son Russell, Mary Russell, my great-grandparents John R. Russell and Delilah Jane Russell, and Calvin B. Russell. Both Calvin's and John R's graves have flat, military stones from the Confederate Army, and Confederate flags move in the breeze next to the stones. Delilah Jane died in 1905 at age sixty-eight, the same year as her daughter Nannie B. Calvin B. Russell died at nineteen, no doubt killed in the Civil War while fighting with the Tennessee Cavalry. John R. Russell, my great grandfather, lived to age eighty-four, marrying again after Delilah Jane's death.

I will find out later that Grandpa Russell took a leading role in the Poplar Ridge community and the Bethel Church.

As I drive away from the cemetery. I think of the broken lamb on the tombstone. In the Victorian era, lambs were often placed on the gravestones of children as a sign of innocence, of a person gone too soon.

Gone too soon. Innocent. My grandmother Nannie B. Russell Chandler was both of these things. She lived less than one year with her new husband, her love.

Perhaps the lamb is also for the little girl she birthed just an hour before she died.

CHAPTER SEVEN

Primitive Baptists

SUNDAY, JUNE 10. I drive in heavy rain to Huntsville to visit with Bledsoe Hereford, one of Lucy's sons. While I hoped he would provide a sense of his mother's life and times, he is somewhat rambling in his talk. I leave soon after tea and cookies. At least I've met one of Lucy's children.

At 6:00, I plan to attend a church service at Bethel Primitive Baptist Church. But first, my grandmother's grave.

By the time I leave Huntsville for the graveyard, the rain has slackened to a drizzle. I arrive earlier than I expected, around 4:30, so I put a rain jacket over my dress, slip on athletic shoes and grab the scrub brush I had purchased the day before to clean off dirt and residue from the gravestones.

My grandmother's stone is free of moss, as are the stones of John R. Russell, my great-grandfather. Grandpa Russell's stone reads, "John R. Russell, Pvt. 2D Co Conf. Inf. Ga Vols, Confederate States Army, 1839 Jan. 23, 1923." His brother, Calvin B. Russell's stone reads, "November 26, 1844 – March 24, 1863, Corporal, Co D in (Holman's) Tennessee Cavalry, Confederate States Army B." I stop to calculate Calvin's age at death—eighteen years old, barely a man.

How do I mourn for this war, for those lost to a cause that I've never believed to be just? What is my legacy? I've come across lists of slaves in my father's line. How do I mourn for the slaves, when some of my kin owned them? I will probably find slave owners among the Russells and the Chapmans. I cannot change history. I can only lament it. I can only hope my ancestors were kind to their slaves.

The stone of my great grandmother, Delilah Jane Russell, is covered with green moss. I kneel down by the stone and scrub over the spots three, four times, until the stone is a bit cleaner that it was before I touched it. I speak to her.

"I wonder if anyone has done this duty for you."

At that moment, I am filled with warmth, peace, connection. I think of the ancestral research I've completed on Delilah's family line, the Chapmans. I traced them back to the Tudor courts of Henry VII and VIII, even to a nanny who watched over Elizabeth I when she was a child. An earlier version of the name was Norman French, *Champernon*, perhaps related to the leaders of the Norman Invasion.

Aristocracy in a rural churchyard in North Alabama. Aristocratic blood possibly ran through the veins of a woman who was all but forgotten after birthing her daughter at age twenty-six, then dying.

***

WHEN I AM FINISHED with Delilah's stone, I drive to Bethel Church for the service. I'm greeted by George Denmark, a man who identifies himself as an elder. He and Elder Ricky Siniard will lead the service.

I introduce myself to Deacon Blackwood, with whom I had spoken on the phone before leaving Michigan. When I called him, his wife answered and said her husband was "out bushhoggin'."

"Bushhogging," I had said. "What a beautiful word! I need to write that one down."

She must have thought it strange that I didn't know that bushhogging is clearing land with a special type of tractor.

I wonder if my farmer ancestors "bushhogged"? I try to imagine it.

The church sanctuary is clean and quiet, the shiny pews graced with floral throws in purple accent. The carpet is purple. I doubt the church where my grandmother worshiped was this colorful.

Before the service begins, I stand talking with the elders and a deacon, as women and men (a total of about fifteen) begin filing into the sanctuary. As each one enters, she or he goes to every person present to shake hands and, in my case, to say her or his name. I enjoy the warm greeting. It seems a wonderful way to "break the ice," so to speak, for a stranger and visitor in the community.

One exception to the handshaking is a woman in light green pantsuit who walks toward me. She has a kind of limp and her body is slightly bent. She's a woman in midlife, probably her fifties. I reach out my hand to her and instead of shaking, she embraces me, putting her arms around my neck.

"So I guess we're not shaking hands," I say.

"I know you. I talked with you on the phone. I'm Ricky Siniard's wife."

I feel blessed by her embrace.

"Of course. Thank you so much for your help in finding Mr. Blackwood."

On the phone, she had given me the number to contact Deacon Blackwood regarding church records.

I tell her my name, though she knows it already, and tell her why I am there, to celebrate my grandmother.

"My name is Syrethia," she says. "What a lovely name!"

The service begins and I sit in the pew behind her. "May I record the service?" I ask.

"Yes," she whispers. "Others used to make recordings."

I thank her and turn on my phone recorder.

Throughout the service, her head turns slightly toward me several times, as if to make sure I'm comfortable.

The first hymn is "The Rock That is Higher Than I," which I later discover comes from Psalms 61:2: "From the end of the earth will I call unto thee, when my heart is overwhelmed: Lead me to the rock that is higher than I."

For days after my return home, the chords of this hymn will ring in my head. I will sing it while I'm brushing my teeth, or driving, even when I am falling asleep.

I think perhaps my search to understand my grandmother has become a kind of "rock" for me.

If I find out about more about her, I think I'll understand my mother.

I'll understand myself.

I realize, as I will tell a Unitarian Universalist congregation when I speak of this trip later in the summer, that "our ancestors aren't going anywhere. We can always find them."

Perhaps finding my ancestors, particularly Grandmother Nannie B. Russell Chandler, is a key to finding and understanding my own sense of incompleteness and rootlessness.

During the service, Ricky Siniard and George Denmark read straight from the Bible. In the case of Primitive Baptists, the label of "primitive" does not mean regressive, as I thought before. It means that these people's worship is "pure" in that it comes straight from the Holy Book, not from theology or from anyone else's ideas.

They each speak for about thirty minutes. They intermingle their personal stories with the chosen readings. I especially appreciate Mr. Denmark's humor. He talks about temptations of the flesh.

"When I go into a store, it's easy for me to walk right past the coolers with beer bottles and cans. But you put a piece of chocolate cake in front of me, I'm lost."

We all laugh, I think, because we all understand that kind of temptation.

The deacon continues. "If you put two pieces of cake in front of me, I know I have to resist because it's not good for my body."

More gentle laughter.

I wonder what these people would think if they knew that later that night, I will open a bottle of wine in my motel room and enjoy a couple of glasses? Would they still welcome me?

At the end of the service, prayers of support are offered for people with trouble. Several members speak of ill friends and neighbors.

When the room becomes silent, I speak.

"I'd like to offer a prayer for my grandmother, Nannie B. Russell Chandler, 1879 to 1905. She was here. She is all but forgotten. I want to find her."

My prayer is accepted as if I'm a member of the congregation. The closing hymn is "Amazing Grace," my mother's favorite.

Just at the end of the service, a heavy rain dashes sheets of water against the side of the church. Everyone waits a few minutes before leaving.

As the rain pounds on the church roof, I chat with Syrethia, asking her to write down her address so that I could thank her and her husband.

"You want me to write it? I think you'd better."

I wonder what she means.

A few minutes later, she tells me she was recently in a major car wreck. She is on many drugs to treat her multiple sclerosis and she temporarily lost control of the car. Now I understood her gait, the odd configuration of her body. I know that disease. My middle sister, Marjorie struggled with it for over thirty years before she died. It is not a noble disease. Yet Syrethia doesn't carry her condition like a burden.

"Please, please be careful in going home! Watch out for other cars!" she cries out as I get in my car.

I feel blessed.

As I back my car out of its spot, she's walking behind me.

"Don't run over me. That wouldn't be good."

She smiles as she waves goodbye.

***

I SPEND THE NEXT WEEK visiting with friends in Birmingham. I return to the church the next Saturday, on my way home to Michigan. I have made an appointment with Mr. Blackwood to look inside a box stored high in a cabinet. He thinks we will find archival church records.

When I arrive for our 9:00 appointment, Mr. Blackwood is waiting. The box is on a table, old manuscripts spread out on one end. They are frayed and yellowed, and I'm almost afraid to touch them.

Some of the records in the middle of the nineteenth century are missing, but Elder Ricky Siniard summarized the activities from 1845 to 1914 in a little book, *Bethel Primitive Baptist Church: History from 1823-1998*. Mr. Blackwood allows me to look through the late nineteenth-century records, when my great grandfather, John R. Russell, was church clerk. I touch the pages where he signed. I take photos of them. I look for references to my grandmother or her sisters and find only one mention of Russell's second wife, Minzie (or Clemanzie, as I will find out later in my research), when she becomes a new church member.

I ask Mr. Blackwood about baptism in this church. He tells me that it happens most often after a person is mature—older than forty. No baptism of babies, nor of school children. No catechism. Just an adult's belief in salvation.

My grandmother was twenty-six when she died. I wonder if she was baptized.

Mr. Blackwood and I examine the church records until around 11 a.m., when he says he needs to leave. I am ready to get on the road, anxious for my seven hundred-mile drive north during which I plan to contemplate all that I've learned and experienced.

I have one more stop, however—Bethel Cemetery. I want to say goodbye to Grandmother Chandler.

Mr. Blackwood drives away in his pickup truck and I head to the cemetery. But I realize Nannie B Russell Chandler's gravestone needs flowers.

I turn my car around and go back toward the church, thinking that I am heading toward New Hope. I see Mr. Blackwood pulling onto the road in his pickup truck, so I flag him down.

"I need to buy some artificial flowers for my grandmother's grave. Can you direct me?"

Mr. Blackwood thinks a moment. "I can lead you toward Huntsville. Will Walmart do? It's about seven miles away."

"Of course it will."

I smile at the irony. I have boycotted Walmart for years because of their bad labor practices. But now, I am happy to go to a Walmart.

Anything for my grandmother.

Blackwood leads me to the store, gets out of his truck, and says, "So are you alright now?"

"Fine" I respond.

We hug and wave goodbye.

One of the repeated statements in the church minutes written by my great-grandfather is "call for the fellowship of the church answered in peace."

That works for me. The faith of my ancestors is not a faith that condemns. It is a faith that includes and loves all those who wish to be in its company. I was loved that Sunday night as I sang and prayed for my grandmother. I was one of them.

After picking out two bunches of blue and purple flowers, I make a swift return to the cemetery. I stand for a few minutes in front of the grave, listening again to the distant engines, the breeze, the birds. I see my mother, a little girl standing in this very spot. I place the flowers in front of the stone, pushing the stems firmly into the ground to make sure they won't blow away in a storm. I want them there when I return even if it's a year from now.

I drive away from the cemetery, thinking of the headless lamb on the tombstone. This beautiful young woman of twenty-six, as the lamb reminds me, left too soon. She left a daughter with a gift of music. Her blood runs in my veins.

Perhaps the lamb is also for me, not dying young, not innocent, but trying to put the pieces back together, to find the missing piece, to complete the story.

Nancy Owen Nelson

Nannie B. Russell Chandler's Dress Buttons.
Recovered from Helen Robinson Paschal,
granddaughter of Mary Russell, Nannie B.'s sister.

CHAPTER EIGHT

Grandma's Buttons[vi]

WHEN I RETURNED from my trip to Alabama, my head spinning with names and charts, visions of the gravestones I'd cleaned, touched, and caressed on that rainy Sunday afternoon. On June 21, I spoke for the first time by phone with my new-found third cousin Helen, Mary Russell's granddaughter.

I located Helen first through Ancestry.com, tracing my grandmother's sister, Mary, through two generations—Mary's daughter Pearl, whom I had met sometime during my childhood. She had rescued me when I was at the Birmingham, Alabama Greyhound Station at age sixteen, deserted by a friend who had promised to pick me up and take me to her college for the weekend. Pearl remained in my memory as the aunt who let me sleep at her apartment after a frightening ride in a taxi through what seemed dangerous, dark city streets. I remembered mostly that she had a fruit salad with coconut, *ambrosia*, my mother called it. A southern dish, I imagined, as I'd only tasted it at family or church gatherings.

Mom had seen Pearl off and on throughout her life. I never knew until I spoke with Helen, Pearl's daughter, now ninety-two years old, about the times when my mother, Nannie B., visited Pearl and her husband "Uncle Dick," Richard Robinson.

Helen said, "Daddy thought your mother was a piece of gold, something handed down from heaven. The first thing he always said when she arrived was, 'Bee, will you play for me?'"

But here is where the family relationships get strange.

Richard was related to my mother only through marriage to Pearl, Mary's daughter and Mom's first cousin. He was the brother of Nannie Dixie Robinson, who had married my grandfather after Nannie B's death. Nannie Dixie was the step-grandmother my sisters and I called "Big Mama." Helen called her "Big Auntie."

So Helen, Pearl, and I were all double-related—one way by blood and one way by marriage.

According to Helen, that didn't matter to her father, Dick. He treated my mother like blood kin.

Helen continued.

"Big Auntie," as Helen called "Big Mama," "did not want anyone to talk to your mother about her mother."

"That's so sad." My voice broke as I fought back the anger rising in my chest.

This was my Big Mama who always represented a warm welcome when we returned from our various places about the country to go "home." And now I saw her in a different light.

How could Big Mama keep my mother from knowing about her mother? How could she live with herself?

For my mother, all of those years of wondering, of feeling something she could not exactly define—this was a reason behind the mystery of why no one would speak of Nannie B. Russell.

I could feel the painful break, a slash in the chain that connected me to my blood grandmother. My mother must have felt it too, but she had no words, no way to define it.

Helen went on to tell a passed-down story of my mother, at three years old, lifted into her father's arms and taken away from Aunt Mary. She was crying.

"He took her away from that family," she said.

The phone call exhausted me. Talking with Helen, I'd envisioned my mother as a young child, crying and being pulled away from her Aunt Mary, the only mother she had known. I'd seen my mother as a young wife with two small girls, visiting Pearl and Helen, lying on the bed and talking endlessly about her mother, stories of Nannie B. Russell's beauty and sweetness passed down from Mary through Pearl to Helen. During our conversation, I recalled my mother in my own life, sometimes becoming sad or reflective, sitting with a cup of coffee, telling me that she never quite fit into this new Chandler family.

Now I comprehend more clearly my mother's feelings of displacement. It helps me to understand my own—always yearning for roots, for belonging, acceptance, and understanding. Why do I long for it so much, even today, when I am challenged by the grasping realities of our world? Why do I need to be "understood," even at this mature time of my life?

It's as if my grandmother, my mother, and I have been floating about, unattached, grasping for something to hold on to. It's as if the world has constantly shifted from the summer day in July 1905, when the young woman gasped and pushed, expelled a baby girl, then bled out. From that day onward, throughout my mother's life of unease in her family, and throughout my life, a constant change of surroundings, always on a quest for something else, that unknown entity—a relationship, fame, perhaps recognition? When will I ever settle into who I am? When will my name become indistinguishable from my life?

During the phone conversation Helen said, "I may have some buttons from your grandmother's clothing in my sewing box. I'll look for them and let you know."

What an extraordinary thought, that I could actually touch, hold buttons that were fastened to Nannie B. Russell's clothes.

I emailed my third cousin Dixie, Helen's granddaughter. We had been communicating since I found her through research.

Dixie promised to look for family photos and share them with me. She also said she would look for the buttons.

A week later, Dixie wrote to me an amusing story about climbing over some loose pipes in Helen's bathroom, dressed in a short skirt, to reach the sewing basket. She took the basket to Helen, who found two buttons fashioned from a pearl-like material, shaped like flowers. She posted a photo on my Facebook wall. They were resting in the palm of her left hand. The photo was fuzzy. And one was chipped.

I did not care. I wanted them.

A few days later, the box arrived via UPS. Inside, the buttons nestled in bubble wrap, each taped carefully all the way around.

I open the package with my grandmother's buttons in the living room. I want to be alone for this intimate encounter with Nannie B. Russell. She touched these, and she wore them on a dress or a blouse.

I walk upstairs to the guest room, where some of my mother's personal items are stored in a drawer from the dresser she inherited from Big Mama. Eleven years ago, I sat on the floor of another guest room in a different house, these pieces of my mother's daily life spread out on the floor. I cried as I cleaned her hairbrush; putting a small bit of hair into a plastic bag. *What if I cloned her?* I thought. *Would she be the same woman, born and raised in a neo-modern time— after women in the workplace had become an ordinary phenomenon, and many women worked even while raising children? Would she look and act the same? Would she somehow bring the same sorrow and loss she suffered in her first birth, into a second one?*

I reach the second floor, open the top drawer of a dresser which, ironically, belonged to Big Mama. I pull out the bag holding my mother's hair. I open the box with Nannie B. Russell's buttons, and then I weave the tendrils of hair around the buttons so that the hair embraces them.

"This is the first time you've touched in 107 years," I say aloud.

Suddenly I feel light-headed, weak and nauseous. I return the buttons and hair to the drawer and lie down on my bed. It's around 11 a.m. Not even lunch time yet.

As I rest, I allow myself to picture my grandmother struggling to give birth. I remember my own struggle in childbirth, sweat running down my face and in my scalp, pressure on my back that I could relieve only by pushing the baby out.

There she is, Nannie B. Chandler Russell, perhaps with her mother Delilah Jane Chapman Russell, or perhaps one of her sisters, Viney, Mary, or Sarah. Her husband Robert is in the next room. Perhaps he paces, or perhaps he sits still and wrings his hands.

Her sister or mother lay cold, wet cloths on Nannie B.'s face. There is a midwife, or a town doctor, who, grim-faced, dips rags into hot water in the corner of the room.

Nannie B. pushes again, and again, gasping in between pushes, her face red and hot with the struggle.

Finally, the baby comes out. It's a little girl. She is small, maybe seven pounds, wrinkled and crying. The doctor wipes the bloody mucous off her wiggling body. He cuts the umbilical cord and hands the baby to her mother.

Robert Chandler enters the room, trying to restrain his excitement, his eyes tearful and his face as red as his wife's.

Nannie B. Russell Chandler looks at her daughter.

"We'll name her for me, Robert?" She says her statement as a question. Robert answers, "Of course, dear. And she will be as beautiful as you are. And she will play the piano and sing, just as you do, to lighten my heart."

Nannie B. smiles, and then she seems to go to sleep. The doctor takes the baby from her arms quickly and gives her to one of the sisters, probably Mary. Mary moves close to the lit fire, cradling the baby. It seems cold in the room, even in the middle of July

"Robert, leave. Now!" The doctor's voice tears into the now quiet room.

"What is it? Is she ill?" The flush on Robert's face deepens.

"Leave the room!"

For the next hour, the doctor works to stanch the blood as it seeps from Nannie B.'s body. He cannot stop it. He cannot wake her.

Finally, he goes to the door and calls Robert.

"I'm sorry. Your wife is slipping away. I can do nothing else to help her."

The tall father kneels by the bed and holds his wife's hand, prays for her to a God he hopes will listen, a God who, from his Primitive Baptist faith, loves rather than condemns, and certainly not the unbaptized baby. Certainly not the mother who dies after she delivers her child.

Soon, the room is silent. The woman's breaths that had come so urgently during the birthing have ceased. The only sound is the weeping of the father.

The buttons are where they belong. Mother and daughter have been apart far too long.

Grandma's Buttons

They adorned her garments,
perhaps on a hot Alabama Sunday
when she walked dirt roads with
her sisters, her mother, her father,
a deacon, to a little church,
simple square building.

Perhaps she sat at the end of a row
halfway down the aisle, fanning
herself as humid air blew through
windows, curtains flashing bright
sunlight as it moved in and out
back and forth, to and from.

Or perhaps the buttons graced
a sweater in winter, underneath
her best warm coat, passed down
from older sisters, not yet worn
enough to make her cold in the
frosty mornings. Then high winds

of January rocked the church windows
seeped through cracks while old
women and children bundled together
leaned toward a stove for warmth.

Perhaps, rather, she wore them
on a silken blouse, this time
her husband next to her,
tall, lanky as his ancestors.

Perhaps as her throat vibrated with
high notes, as her chest rose to take
In breath, fell to release it with music,
perhaps then the buttons moved up
and down, kept rhythm on her breast.

Once she wore them, my grandmother,
on a blouse, or smock. pearled flowers
smoothed by time and touched
by fingers stroking lovely petals.

7/24/12

Big Mama—Nannie Dixie Robinson Chandler,
Second Wife of Robert E. Chandler,
stepmother to Nannie B. Chandler Nelson,
and step-grandmother to the author

CHAPTER NINE

Robinson

WHEN I SPOKE TO HELEN on June 21, I recorded our conversation with her permission. Her voice was spirited and lively.

She was ninety-two. Only months later, in March, 2013, she would die from a stroke.

We talk again about my mother, called by Helen and others "Bee," about how she visited often, always wanting to hear Pearl, Helen's mother, tell her what she knew about her own mother.

"My dad (Richard Robinson, known through family talk as "Grandpa Robinson") loved her. He thought she was something handed down from heaven."

"I did too," I say, as always, wishing I could have been more aware or appreciative of my mother before I lost her.

"Bee was an outgoing person. She loved everybody," adds Helen.

Many of my memories of my mother are edged with irritation, a sense of competition between us. Nannie B. Chandler Nelson knew how to engage people, how to charm them, make them feel special. I, on the other hand, was the class nerd, I thought, with my Honors Society membership, short haircut, and constant studying. I had friends, but I didn't see myself as "charming," but more insular, self-conscious, eager to please.

Searching for Nannie B.

I felt relieved in some ways when, in 1964, I left home for Birmingham-Southern. I was relieved because I could escape the little town of Hartselle. I was not like the other kids. Most of my classmates had been born and raised there, had gone to school together from kindergarten through senior year of high school. I had moved to Hartselle when I was fourteen, ready for high school. Unlike others around me, I had traveled and changed schools, learned about different cultures. Yet generations of my ancestors had lived, farmed, married, and had children in this town. They helped establish the First Methodist Church. In Hartselle, I felt as if I was under a microscope. I was identified with my grandparents and even earlier ancestors in my family, ready to carve out my separate identity. College would give me a chance to figure out who I was as an individual. I was the only one of my sisters who went to college. I would prove that I could achieve through my studies. I had no idea what would happen after that.

When the time came for me to leave, though, I was sad. The night before we were to drive to Birmingham in two cars, packed to the roofs with my towels, bed sheets, clothes, shoes, and books, my mother came into my room and sat on the end of the bed. She began to cry. Soon her crying turned to sobbing. I'd never seen her that way before. I felt sick inside, as if somehow, I was abandoning her. How could I stay in this small town? I had broken up with my handsome track star boyfriend, Jerry, because I felt trapped. On some level, I knew staying with him would confine me. Most of my life I had traveled around, seen new places and met new people. I wasn't ready to stay put, marry, and have babies, as many of my high school classmates planned to do. I longed for a bigger world.

My bedroom was dark that night, and we just sat there for a while on my bed, my mother sobbing. I don't recall crying myself, but I do recall feeling as if I had some very important artifact, like cut glass or crystal, in my hand, and that, as I often felt with my father, it would break if I did not take care to hold it, cherish it, wrap it for safekeeping. I was afraid of losing or breaking what I had with my mother. Yet I was also afraid of losing myself.

What I didn't understand at the time was that my mother was grieving the loss of her last daughter, the one who came late, the "surprise" baby. She was losing, she probably thought, the one daughter who shared her passions of literature, poetry, languages, who had studied Latin for two years in high school and who would be taking French in her first quarter of college. She was losing the daughter who sang with her in the church choir and took piano lessons from Aunt Lois, my Dad's older sister.

My mother must have felt that this was one more loss. Her mother, and now her youngest daughter.

***

THERE WERE TIMES during my childhood when I felt that I had not lived up to my mother's expectations. I remember one visit to Hartselle from "Aunt Pearl," Helen's mother. Mom asked me to play the piano, which I did to please her. I don't remember what song, but my playing was awful. I'd never had the natural penchant for playing for an audience, like Mom did. I wasn't confident, played haltingly. My mother found the music in the piano keys. When she played, it was magic. She seemed to play with no effort, the music flowing from the tips of her fingers.

That day when I made a mess of a simple song on the piano, I recall that Pearl said something like "Oh," when I finished. It sounded like a sigh of displeasure or disappointment. After a few awkward moments, the conversation resumed. I don't remember whether I stayed or left the living room. All I do remember is my embarrassment about my horrible playing.

Sitting at the piano was one place where I could not excel, even though I had played during my high school graduation ceremony. I remember that I missed a chord or two. They should have asked Mom to play.

During our phone conversation, Helen keeps talking about Mom's playing the piano and how much Helen's father, Richard Robinson, loved to hear her play.

Was Helen in the room when I played the piano that day in Hartselle?

On the day when they visited, I had little interest in this strange part of the family, the Russells and Robinsons, who seemed only to have the flimsiest kinship with us. They were not Nelsons or Chandlers, or anyone related to those families. So why should I be concerned about them?

Now, some fifty years later, I am talking with Pearl's daughter Helen, who says to me several times during our talk, "I lost everyone. Now I found a part of my family. I found you."

Helen was my only living link to my biological grandmother, Nannie B. Russell Chandler.

***

"SHE WAS JEALOUS of his first marriage. She knew he loved Aunt Nannie B. But listen, she [Nannie B.] was gone and she [Nannie Dixie] got him." Helen is talking about my step-grandmother, Nannie Dixie Robinson Chandler, the woman Grandpa Chandler married less than three years after my grandmother's death.

Then Helen speaks about Nannie B.'s baby, my mother.

"When Uncle Ed (Robert Chandler) married again, he took her away from that family.... I'd always heard [Nannie B. Russell Chandler] died at [childbirth]. My mother said she was so pretty. My grandmother kept her [the baby] for five years. You know, my grandmother about died when they came to get her."

Helen's dates are wrong. Robert E. Chandler married Nannie Dixie Robinson Chandler on April 19, 1908—three years, not five, after his first wife's death. Some time after that date, he and his new wife picked up my mother, Nannie B. Chandler, a little girl of three. But in our conversation, Helen pulled no punches about what she was told had happened over a hundred years ago. As she had several times before, she described my mother, a little girl, crying and holding out her arms to Aunt Mary. She didn't want to leave the only mother she'd known.

74

"How can you be jealous of a dead person?" I ask Helen.

"She felt she wasn't getting the attention."

Amazing. Nannie Dixie and Robert had five children (one girl died) in the next ten years, then a boy much later, a small number compared to some of the farm families I've seen on Ancestry.com who produced ten children in the same period. Still, Nannie and Robert had babies. They were together. In fact, my mother used to laugh and say that when her father and his wife went into their bedroom after lunch for "rest time," it was understood that no one disturb them.

Big Mama got plenty of attention.

Helen and I talk again about the kinship which exists between Helen's father (Big Mama's brother) and Helen's mother Pearl (Nannie B's sister, Mary's daughter), which has resulted in our being doubly-related. Helen loves how her father and mother met and married.

"That's something positive that came out of all of this," I say.

"Yes, it is."

Of course it is. Helen would not be here. Nor would her granddaughter, Dixie, who is named after Big Mama (Nannie Dixie). It was Dixie who retrieved and mailed me the buttons.

Without the Robinson line, I would not have the buttons. There would be no buttons to join with her daughter's hair. There would be no memories passed down. No reunion.

***

WHEN I FOUND OUT at age twelve that Big Mama was not my grandmother, for a time I felt confused. For a while after that conversation with Mom, I was angry. *Why hadn't anyone told me this before? Is Mom protecting me, or herself?*

I had to make an adjustment about how I viewed my family. I don't remember how I felt when I saw Big Mama the first time after I learned the truth about my biological grandmother. I must have thought about what I had learned. I don't recall feeling any different during our visits to her home in Decatur, Alabama.

Nannie Dixie Robinson, "Big Mama," had her own challenges after she married Robert. Not only did she have a stepdaughter, but one of her daughters, Mildred, died from colitis. Another daughter, Frances, a superb vocalist, was shot to death by her estranged husband in a hospital parking lot in Houston, Texas. Then he shot himself, all in the presence of Frances' son, Tommy. If I include Tommy and my mother, Big Mama nurtured eight children.

In many ways, Big Mama fulfilled the image of the delicate Southern lady. I can see her fanning herself in her rocker. When she tired, I'm told, she would admit herself to the local hospital for bed rest, much as a Southern belle might "swoon" at anything unsettling. When alarmed, Big Mama would ask for smelling salts, and in her later years, I remember that she and her tenant Mrs. Morris would lament how the young people were "going to the dogs," or "going to pot," mildly ironic, especially the last statement.

Big Mama proved to be strong and resilient. When her husband, Grandpa Robert Chandler, died of cancer in his early fifties, her children expected her to fold into her grief. Instead, she put on her business dress, got in her car, and drove to Robert Chandler's dry goods store on Second Avenue, in Old Decatur, to take over the management of the business. As a response to the murder of her daughter Frances, she took in Frances' son, Tommy.

I try to understand why she would be jealous of my grandmother. After all, she had my grandfather for decades, as well as a house and children. Until Mom told me the truth that afternoon when I was thirteen, as far as I was concerned, Big Mama *was* my grandmother. She maintained a home where all of her family was welcome. When I was very small, while we were waiting for news from Dad about when we would move to Alaska, we rented a house about a block and a half down the street. Hers was a second home for me that summer of 1950.

I have a sweet memory of wandering outside of our house on Fourth Avenue, in Decatur. I often smelled something sweet, like lilacs, or dogwood. I balanced myself as I walk along the edge of the cement border about a foot high, which surrounded our yard. I ran next door to say hi to the Goodes, whose little dog Brownie was my friend. Then I would probably get my best friend Bobby and we would walk down one block to Big Mama's where she would be sitting on the porch with Mrs. Morris. As we approached, both women would exclaim, making the familiar cooing sound in their throats, "Well lawsy mercy, there's that sweet Nancy. . . and her friend Bobby!" They'd give us cookies, or perhaps in her apartment downstairs, Mrs. Morris would fix us some peanut butter spread on crackers.

I spent many happy hours in Big Mama's house, eating her food and rocking on the big front porch while I watched cars drive slowly past the house.

Talking with Helen about "Big Auntie's" jealousy of Nannie B. Russell, I felt anger toward Big Mama that she did not encourage my mother to know about Nannie B. I see it as a robbery of sorts that set my mother on a course of guilt and loss that she felt until her death. Yet I hear from my sister Betty that when I was born, Big Mama made the bus trip of thousands of miles from Decatur, Alabama to Fort Lewis, Washington. She told my mother when she arrived that she treated all of the bus drivers like her sons. I imagine they treated her like a mother.

Betty recently sent me a small sepia photo of Nannie Dixie. The caption, written by my mother, reads "Victoria, B. C. Big Mama in Empress Hotel Gardens." On the back is written "June, 1946." This was just around the time of my birth, when Nannie took my sisters Marge and Betty into Canada so that Mom could have time to settle in with me. In the photo, she stands in a sweater and skirt, a bonnet on her head, behind tall flowers. I can barely make out the flower decoration on the hat. She holds her purse on her left arm. She is very much a proper southern lady. And she is the only grandmother I knew.

Even if Nannie Dixie was jealous of her first husband's dead wife, she created a home for me in the midst of a life of travel and change in the military. I can still honor her for what she was and did. That will not take away from my search to understand my *real* grandmother.

When I see Big Mama's framed photo in the family gallery on my wall, I see the face of a kind and loving woman, her hair pulled back to show a solid bone structure, a square jaw, a well-shaped face. I remember the slow and quiet afternoons on her front porch, listening to the crickets or watching the faces of pansies as they fluttered in the hot summer breeze. I remember eating a meatloaf and ketchup sandwich in her cool kitchen, while her black friend and helper, Aunt Mandie, hummed nearby, or taking a nap in the back bedroom, a swivel fan lightly whispering while the afternoon heat peaked before the cooling evening.

And I realize again that I have Nannie B. Russell's buttons *because of,* not in spite of, Nannie Dixie Robinson.

SECOND AVENUE (SOUTH END) — NEW DECATUR.

Robert E Chandler's store in Decatur, Alabama was located on Second Avenue. This is how it would have looked at the turn to the Twentieth Century.

(Property of Morgan County Historical Archives, Decatur, AL.)

A Stylish Nannie B. Chandler of the 1920s

CHAPTER TEN
Mother's Day

MAY 12, 2013. At 9:00 this morning, I enter First Unitarian Universalist Church of Detroit and climb onto the platform where the choir practices. I'm early, and our director, Todd, plays the recorded background for today's song, "Flying Free," which speaks to the ability to face darkness and pain to "fly free" within the beauty of life. Some other choir members hum their parts. Above us, the pipe organs rise to the ceiling, and sunlight glints through the stained glass windows behind the organ. It was constructed by Ernest M. Skinner and is almost a hundred years old.

We are a small choir, at most eleven or twelve people. As we warm up, our voices begin to blend, the chords echoing off of the high neo-gothic arches in the ceiling.

Near the end of practice, the church secretary brings me notes from my minister, Roger Mohr. This morning I am to share the homily with him. The title is "Our Feminist Faith."[vii] A day or so ago, I prepared my part of the program by collecting passages from women writers who were Unitarians or Universalists. As I searched, I marveled at the strong messages of empowerment and voice in these writings.

The first woman I selected was Abigail Adams, wife of John Adams, second president of the United States, who, as early as 1776, wrote in a letter to her husband to "Remember the Ladies" in founding the country. *Remember what about them?* I wondered. In her case, she warns her husband not to let the laws of the new nation "put such unlimited power into the hands of the Husbands," *but what else must be remembered?* Women's right to fulfill their talents in the world, and not necessarily at home, raising children, or, as Mary Wollstonecraft writes, to be more than "gentle, domestic brutes"? Their right to vote and hold office, to change the course of community and nation? Their right to be the "arbiter[s]" of their own destinies, as Elizabeth Cady Stanton says to the U. S. Congress in 1872? The ability to "become" themselves, words from May Sarton in "Now I Become Myself": "My work, my love, my time, my face / Gathered into one intense / Gesture of growing like a plant"?

My mother loved May Sarton. In her copy of *Selected Poems by Mary Sarton,* she had jotted down page numbers of several poems at the top of the title page. It was her habit to mark passages and reflect on the poetry, often writing commentary in the margins. On page 191, "Now I Become Myself," she boxed in the title with pencil. She underlined and embraced these lines at the end of the poem with parentheses, as follows:

> *So all the poem is, can give,*
> *Grows in me to become the song,*
> *Made so and rooted by love.*
> *Now there is time and Time is young.*
> *(O, in this single hour I live)*
> *(All of myself and do not move.)*
> *(I, the pursued, who madly ran,)*
> *(Stand still, stand still, and stop the sun!)*

Sarton's lines are *not* those of a woman whose life is controlled by others. They are words of a woman who wants to "seize the day" and create poems and songs. To have a voice.

My mother wrote poetry for years—mostly rhymed, with simple metaphors, definitely not in contemporary style or form. She published in the Alabama Poetry Society journal, *The Sampler.* She never ventured into the big world of publishing. She read and wrote poetry to deal with her internal conflicts.

I have a bound notebook of my mother's poetry. Many of the poems are about her daily struggles with depression, friendships, loneliness, and grieving for my father. Without her biological mother, she spent her life searching for voice—in music, in writing, in her life with her husband. As did Sarton, she did her best to "not move" from the task.

During the service I am to read select passages from a second podium. The minister, Reverend Mohr, has chosen them and will comment on each passage as it reflects notions of our liberal faith. As usual, my heart pounds faster as I anticipate speaking publicly.

I've done this a hundred times. Yet I always feel nervous about doing a good job, not blundering, not fumbling to get the words out.

The service begins.

First, I read from Abigail Adam's letter to her husband on March 31, 1776, on the eve of the formation of our nation. After asking that he "remember the ladies," she assures John that women will "foment a rebelion [sic]" if they are not treated well. John replies on April 5 that the men will not be subject to the "tyranny of the Peticoat [sic]," to which Abigail replies on May7 that "we have it in our power not only to free ourselves but to subdue our Masters." As always, when I review the letters between these two, I wonder what happened to Abigail's insistence on equality and generous treatment. Why did it disappear into the annals of history in books written by men?

Our minister speaks about the letters and then asks me to read from Mary Wollstonecraft, *Vindication of the Rights of Women*. She writes of men's efforts to keep women "in a state of childhood" to assure women's "good conduct." Reverend Mohr talks about bearing children—its necessity for the human race, but also its use by some men as a method of controlling women, keeping them in the home and out of the world.

He speaks of the importance of "individual happiness and development" for both genders.

Searching for Nannie B.

He moves to a point that hits home for me: "at one time the leading cause of death for women early in their lives was childbearing … It's terminal."[viii]

I think of my grandmother and her death at age twenty-six, one hour after birthing little Nannie B. I think of the gravestone, with incorrect spelling of her name, blank of any signs of love or connection. I think of my mother, Nannie B. Chandler Nelson, whose life was directed from its earliest hours by the absence of her biological mother.

What did the newborn, my mother, eat? Did my grandfather hire a nursemaid? Did Aunt Mary, Nannie B. Russell's sister, use cow milk or cereal and water (as they sometimes did in the early twentieth century) for the newborn? At what point was it decided that Nannie B.'s sister, Mary, would take and care for the baby?

My grandfather, though not wealthy, later earned a comfortable income because of his mercantile store at the corner of Second Avenue and Moulton, in Decatur, Alabama. The 1910 U. S. Census, only five years after his first wife's death, lists him as a "merchant" with a "clothing store." Certainly he would have had the money to help his sister-in-law pay for a nursemaid.

My mind travels back to the service. Next I am to read Charlotte Perkins Gilman, the author of "The Yellow Wallpaper," about a woman whose husband, a doctor, ordered the "rest cure" for her malady, which he associated with sickness caused by writing. Ultimately, she goes mad and sees a woman crawling inside the yellow wallpaper. This woman is trying desperately to free herself from her husband's entrapment.

I understand this character's panic at being kept in, away from her real life of writing, her voice. When I married the first time while in college, I found myself walking through every room in our student apartment. I kept thinking I should be doing something, anything, significant, out in the world. Yet I planned meals far in advance and made sure the vacuuming and laundry were done, the towels folded neatly and put away.

I had been Valedictorian of my high school class. I would be awarded membership in Phi Theta Kappa Honorary Society at my college graduation. And yet, like Gilman's character, between periods of studying, I restlessly walked through the two-room apartment, checking everything for domestic perfection. Like Gilman's protagonist, I could have gone mad. Until my dad told me "Get out of that apartment! Get a job!" He was wiser than I realized at the time. He understood my need for empowerment.

After more words from Reverend Mohr, I read words from Elizabeth Cady Stanton, a "mother" of women's suffrage; she delivered the "Declaration of Sentiments" at the first Women's Civil Rights Conference in Seneca, New York. She writes of the importance of a woman as "an equal factor in civilization, her rights and duties are still the same-individual happiness and development."

Against the odds of a life as military spouse, my mother created her own individual happiness and development. She created a life wherever we moved. She wrote poetry from her college years until her death. Her notebook of poetry contains most of these poems. Mom wrote about the frozen river she walked over in Fairbanks, Alaska with a general's wife, Mrs. Hood—poems about her friendships, about illness, about her despair over not being able to write. In one poem, "Within Me," she writes of her "Judas, who smiling, dares to squelch / my confidence / and my desire for creation." There is no date on the poem. This could have been written any time during her life, any period when she was struggling to find voice.

As Reverend Mohr makes his closing remarks, I think again of the lives of the two women who came before me; one whose life was cut short in childbirth, the other who struggled to find her voice in the world even as she committed to a life of travel, of childbearing, and of being, as she used to say, "just a housewife."

Did my mother ever experience the "transcendence" of gender that my minister talks about? I'm not sure. She did what she could under the circumstances. She was a "Mrs." either during or soon after the publication of the *Morcohi, Volume IV, 1928,* annual. She never worked full time again after that year of high school teaching. I'm sure she wanted to, despite her protestation that she wouldn't like the "red tape" of teaching. I'm sure because she never stopped teaching in the various places she lived—as a substitute, and later in life as a tutor of English grammar, or a teacher of French or Latin. Only after her death did I find out that she never charged a penny for any of those lessons.

I also know that during the years I was with her, she would sigh and say, "It's a man's world." Even in my youth, this statement made me recoil. I hated it. As I progressed through my education and in and out of marriages, I responded with something like, "I don't think so any more, Mom. I think women are coming into their own." *After all*, I thought, *you decided to give up everything for Dad. You chose to let it be a man's world.*

After these conversations, I was usually very irritated. I was determined to do better. I was determined to move the game piece forward.

The homily ends with my reading of the May Sarton poem, "Now I Become Myself." I try to enunciate carefully, despite static feedback I get from the microphone when use d's or t's. I move back just far enough, but not too far away, in order to render the words clearly. Like many issues in life, this position at the microphone is delicate and takes attention and consideration.

> *Now I become myself. It's taken*
> *Time, many years and places;*
> *I have been dissolved and shaken,*
> *Worn other people's faces,*
> *Run madly, as if Time were there,*
> *Terribly old, crying a warning,*
> *'Hurry, you will be dead before-*
> *(What? Before you reach the morning?*
> *Or the end of the poem is clear?*
> *Or love safe in the walled city?)*

How many times since my retirement from full-time teaching have I felt that I was just waiting to die? Like Sarton, I have "run madly," trying both to find a rock-solid place and pushing away the notion of death as if it were pursuing me. Here is the answer in Sarton's poem.

> *The black shadow on the paper*
> *Is my hand; the shadow of a word*
> *As thought shapes the shaper*
> *Falls heavy on the page, is heard*
> *All fuses now, falls into place*
> *From wish to action, word to silence,*
> *My work, my love, my time, my face*
> *Gathered into one intense*
> *Gesture of growing like a plant.*

This work before me, these "shadows" of words I've been writing about my grandmother and mother, grow inside me "like a plant." I will continue to write their stories. With help from my research, from the interviews I've gathered about my grandmother, I will imagine the life of a woman who died in childbirth. Finding that truth, I will understand, in a way I never have before, the woman who birthed me.

CHAPTER ELEVEN

"Miss, or Mrs.?"

THIS QUESTION ASKED by the students in the *Morcohi* yearbook would become my question as I grew into adulthood. I recall a period during my undergraduate years at Birmingham Southern college, early in 1965, when I was struggling with depression. It was soon after I arrived at college and I was still feeling lonely and confused. I didn't know where I was going with my life. I went to see my advisor, Dr. Baxter, who handed me a copy of Betty Friedan's *The Feminine Mystique*.

"This book may give you some help in figuring out your way, Nancy."

I climbed the hill to Hanson Dorm, wondering how the book in my hand could change me.

As I look back on that moment, I marvel that a professor at a Methodist college in the South would have been so wise. It was the 1960s for God's sake. How could a *man* in Dr. Baxter's position advise a young woman to read Friedan's groundbreaking work and to look realistically at the traditional path of marriage and family, to think of her own personal goals first?

This was before I married my first husband in 1966. Only months after the wedding, the Anglican priest who married us asked us, "Do you remember God said in the Bible, 'Be fruitful and multiply'?"

At that moment, I recoiled, as if someone had cast a net over my body. I could feel my spirit flailing and thrashing, trying to remove the net of obligation. Why must I have children immediately, or at all? I was in college and wanted to finish my degree. I wanted to pursue a professional life of some kind. I wanted to distinguish myself from my sisters, and even from my mother, who never had a chance to explore any possibility but marriage and family.

After my first divorce and my affair with a college professor in the early 1970s, I became a feminist caught up in the notions of equal rights, respect on the job, and consciousness-raising groups. This happened subtly, over a period of time. The question shifted to "Am I Ms., not Miss, or Mrs."? As years passed, I would marry a total of four more times. I had taken my first husband's name and would take my second husband's. I would wrestle with my identity in society. What would I accomplish? Would I be an academic? A teacher and scholar? Would I be empowered? This was during the sometimes fractious '60s and '70s feminist movement; the Betty Friedans of the world had turned society on its head. Feminists were marching, burning bras. I wasn't one of those bra-burners, but I felt changes within myself that I did not articulate. I feared disappearing. I asked myself, *Should I vanish under the name of Mrs. Somebody? Or could I remain Ms., the feminist label for women who did not want to be identified by marital status?*

As I look back on this period in my life, I see a connection to my family and my birth. I was a late-born child, coming into a family with two teenagers. Both of my older sisters chose marriage over college and life-long professions. However, both of our parents went to college. Why would my sisters not go to college when they were raised by college-educated parents?

I felt I needed to go further than my sisters, perhaps even further than my parents—get the advanced degrees, teach in college, write and publish. I would do what my mother had not been able to do. I wanted to please both of my parents. I would do better than they had. I would make up for something that was missing. I just didn't know what.

Searching for Nannie B.

As I moved through college, out of a marriage and into graduate school, then into another marriage, I felt myself pulling away from this impulse to walk the traditional path. In an interim from grad school when I worked for the Jefferson County, Alabama Commission, I worked on voter registration before a local election. I had married again, and I signed my name "Nancy Nelson (plus my second husband's last name)," my fingers often cramping in the process, as if they resisted writing the name. By the end of voter registration, my hands ached with signing my three names. I did not know that decades later, I would choose to be known only by my birth name, *Nancy Owen Nelson*. I didn't know that when I signed my full, real name, it would be with a looping between the "y" in "Nancy" and the "O" in "Owen. The names would merge into one identity, one gesture of writing. I only knew that the three names I was signing then seemed tedious, unnecessary.

It was during this second marriage when I turned the corner toward my professional development. Near time for graduation with my Ph.D., Bill and I decided to look for jobs in Michigan. We had a friend in the Detroit area, and I had lived in the Upper Peninsula during my dad's last military assignment. I loved what I remembered of the ethos of Michigan, at least in the U.P.—vast forest land, lakes, an international flavor.

I was the first of us to get a job. The English Department at Albion College, a private Methodist college much like Birmingham Southern, needed a sabbatical replacement for one year. Why not try it? I thought.

When I accepted the job, it was weeks before I was to graduate from Auburn with a doctorate in English. Before the graduation ceremony, my mother and I drove from Alabama to Michigan in a VW Beetle, with two cats and a load of silverware and other household items. Several days later, we would fly back to Auburn for graduation. On the trip north, we stayed in a motel outside of Indianapolis. It turned out to be a fleabag. The cats stayed in the room with us, and when I opened the door for some reason, both of them ran out into the hallway. I can still see my seventy-five-year old mother walking rapidly down the hall calling "Tonto! Yoyo!" against the sounds of drunken laughter in the rooms near us.

My valiant mom, up for anything.

During the night, someone broke into the VW. Nothing was stolen, but Mom and I got out of the motel as swiftly as possible.

Again my mother was there for me. She considered the trip an adventure, and it didn't disappoint her.

***

AFTER GRADUATION, Bill and I settled into a rented house in the small town of Albion. I made friends quickly in the English Department. Two of the women would become godmothers to my son when he was born a year later, in the fall of 1980.

My marriage worsened during this year. My desire for a baby did not help a troubled marriage. In a way, I was moving along the traditional path of marriage and children, but I wanted more. I had earned my degree and I wanted a professional life. I wanted it all. Had I felt cut out for the traditional path, things would probably been all right. After all, I knew how to be domestic.

While we were in Albion, I made all of our bread from scratch for an entire year. Perhaps from the outside I looked as if I was going to be a mother, and only a mother. But forget about this PhD business! After teaching and taking classes for almost a decade, writing papers, three years of immersion in my dissertation topic on female stereotypes in the novels of Tobias Smollett, how could Bill think I would abandon my work? This was who I was—an academic *and* a mother. Both roles were essential to who I was.

It became evident that the marriage was not going to accommodate my desire to "have it all." But I had no plan. After one year, my job at Albion was finished. I had applied for a job at a community college near Detroit.

The summer seemed interminable. For a long time, we had no phone. I was in limbo with a nine-month-old baby, no job, no friends to speak of.

After a phone line was installed, I received a call from the department chair at the college. I had been selected for an interview. Something told me I was on my way.

When my divorce went through in the summer of 1982, I was Nancy Owen Nelson, PhD. That would be my identity. Forever.

Yet still, after all these years and all of my marriages, the idea of male dominance makes my stomach turn. Earning a PhD should have proven my identity and my worth.

My mother must have felt the same entrapment. She never talked about it, and she was stalwart in fulfilling her role as a military wife, stoic in dealing with dad's drinking. But I remember that she also loved May Sarton. My mother wanted a voice. The signing of her many different versions of her name on her music and in the *Morcohi* annual suggests confusion, the same confusion I felt and still sometimes feel about my identity.

Who am I? I'm a mother, a wife, a teacher, a friend. What is my core?

I'm sure the baby Nannie B. Chandler must have felt the rhythms of her life interrupted by the cutting of the cord between her birth mother and herself.

When I had a miscarriage in my early twenties after an affair with a professor, I did not think of my mother and my grandmother. The fetus was only six or seven weeks along.

When I was pregnant with my son, and despite any problems in the marriage, I was filled with a sense of awe at the changes in my body. In the later months I would lie on the living floor and watch my huge belly rise and fall. I would feel the movement of the baby, like butterfly wings, inside me. During the birth, my only fear was that I would have to have a Caesarean section. When the baby emerged from me, I told the nurses between gasps of relief that this birth was a miracle. They smiled and nodded.

Not once did I fear for my life or that of my son.

Not once did the thought of my grandmother's struggle and death in childbirth cross my mind.

These issues have not resolved themselves, for me or for other women. I see our country sliding backward in terms of women's rights. During the last election year, Republican candidates worked against contraceptive coverage on insurance policies, and a major right-wing radio voice called a young graduate student who was advocating for birth control a "slut" and worse. It's as if a machismo tiger has been let loose, his teeth dripping with the blood of feminists.

In my classrooms, few students know about the suffragettes' fight for the vote early in the twentieth century. Many think "feminist" is a dirty word.

I am often addressed in businesses as a *girl* or a *lady*, instead of a woman. What's the matter with lady? I suppose nothing, if used by an intimate friend, but the word carries with it the aristocratic label of proper etiquette and social behavior, a type of "goodness," a pattern I broke after my father died. "Lady" suggests a controlled creature, a woman whose voice is not heard. The woman who crawls inside the yellow wallpaper of Charlotte Perkins Gilman's story by the same name—she was a lady who drifted into insanity when her voice was not heard.

Most annoying to me are the people who don't understand why my name is different from my husband's. On a recent radio talk show, I heard someone refer to the women who kept their names as "a thing of the 1970s."

Are we indeed moving backward? Why would anyone want to hide under someone else's identity? My name as given at birth already has the names of men in my ancestry, the Owens and the Nelsons. "Nancy" was my grandmother's name (Nancy Jane Owen, as I discovered on Ancestry. com). I've always felt blessed to carry her name while my sisters were named after a blouse label and a doll.

Perhaps my parents named me for my great-grandmother for a reason. I always felt that they had a special purpose in mind for me. There was my father's pride in my accomplishments, and there was my mother's and my shared love of teaching and literature.

In her own way, my mother was a feminist. She never lived independently or earned a living. She never worked after the year before she married. Yet she was always distinct in her personhood. Wounded by early loss, she defined herself during both her marriage and her widowhood.

She would live thirty-four years after my dad died. She would not remarry. She would teach and read and study. She would be loved and remembered by many.

Nancy Owen Nelson

Robert Goodman and Nancy Jane Thomason Owen with an unidentified baby, possibly a grandchild—aunt or uncle of the author. The photo was probably taken in the 1920s. The author, daughter of Nannie B. Chandler, is named after this grandmother on her father's side of the family.

CHAPTER TWELVE
Being Nancy Owen Nelson

"ARE YOU NANCY WILSON, or Olsen, or Owen?"

"No, I'm Nancy Owen Nelson."

"I'm unable to find your name in our conference registration records. Oh, never mind. Here you are. I put it under 'O.' Isn't your name hyphenated?" "No, it's Nancy Owen Nelson, no hyphens. It is my birth name." *Blank look.*

"Sorry. I'm glad we found you."

OR

A piece of mail comes for my husband, Roger Zeigler. It's addressed to "Mr. Roger Nelson." Apparently, no one can imagine that my husband and I do not share a last name.

I want to say, "Why should I take a man's name and disappear?"

I want to say, "Why don't men take their wives' names?" (Some men do hyphenate their last names with their wives').

I have a name I will keep forever.

From my earliest memory, I knew that I was named after a special woman, my great grandmother, Nancy Jane Thomasson Owen, wife of my great grandfather, Robert Goodman Owen. To reinforce the special honor, I inherited three items that belonged to her—a trunk from the Civil War era, a cut glass pickle dish, and a china sugar bowl with a chipped top. I have taken these treasures with me for all of my moves since leaving home. I refinished the trunk while I was pregnant with my son, whom I named Owen. The trunk is a symbol of family lineage. I felt that being named after Nancy was a special action on my parents' part, like being crowned or knighted. I'm not sure why I felt that way, except that Dad always spoke of his grandmother with warmth. Everyone else who knew her spoke of her with something close to awe. They called her "Mammie Owen." I discovered only recently that she taught Sunday school for forty years in the same Methodist church that her son-in-law, Steve Nelson, had helped to build, the same church where generations of family followed her, where her grandson, my father, Owen Nelson, had taught Sunday School in his later years, and where I married my first husband. That was the first time I took someone else's name.

Nancy Jane Thomasson Owen died in 1933, four years after her husband Robert died in front of a train, in downtown Hartselle. I'd heard this piece of family lore about his violent death, but it had not stayed with me for some reason, perhaps because no one ever said, or perhaps knew, why he died in this violent way. A news article from *The Hartselle Enterprise* of October 31, 1929, states that he was "blinded by the light" of the train's engine. Since it was a Saturday evening at 6:00 p.m., it was likely dark when the train approached. "Daddy Owen," as he was called, was deaf, and perhaps he did not hear the train. He was thrown several feet, and his injuries included a hole in the side, cracked ribs, and "minor injuries."

In the late evening, he died in his home.

Why, really, did he step in front of a train? If it was dark, why wouldn't he see the light of the oncoming engine?

The stock market crash that began the Great Depression happened only days before, on October 24. The 1920 U. S. Census lists Robert Goodman as a "cotton buyer." Either I never knew this, or I forgot it, until I saw it on the census. Ironically, my father also worked as a cotton buyer both early in his marriage and as his last job after retirement from the U. S. Army.

I have no way of knowing whether my great-grandfather lost investments on that dark day in American history.

Apparently, Robert Goodman Owen cut an impressive figure. His obituary describes him as "a man of splendid physic ... [with] snowy white hair and mustache." Chris Hanlin, a historian on the Owen side, sent me a photo of four of the Owen siblings. The man on the far left has a white mustache and white hair. It must be Robert, though the photo was not labeled.

When I saw it, I realized I had seen a picture of my great grandfather some time in my life. I couldn't remember where, but I knew the face.

Another photo from Chris is of the same white-mustachioed man with a small, white-haired woman who is probably Nancy on his left. He is on the main level of a sidewalk, probably in front of a house. She is standing one step up. If the woman had not stood on the step, she would have appeared like a child next to the tall man.

Robert is holding an unidentified infant. He is squinting into the sun, but Nancy has a slight smile on her face. Hers is not a look of absolute joy, despite the fact that her husband is holding a baby who is probably a grandchild. Rather, it is a smile that barely lifts her cheeks upward. She is looking at the baby.

Nancy wears a dark dress with a matronly cut. Her hands are behind the dress. She seems modest, proper. I have trouble merging the image in this photograph of a proper southern lady with the story that she poured warm urine into the ears of her children to treat their earaches.

In this writing, I have been concerned about names, about identity and empowerment, for my grandmother, my mother, and myself. Yet here is my name—the first from a woman who, most likely, never thought about being empowered. Nancy Owen's only focus in life must have been her husband and family. Her other names, Jane and Thomassen, have no relevance to my naming. In fact, I would not have known them if I had not done research into family history.

My second, middle name, "Owen," also defines me. It's the name people have the most trouble with because "Nancy Nelson" is easy to say, list, remember, but "Nancy Owen Nelson" is trouble; it's complicated. "Owen," of course, comes from Robert's family name—the name of people who came from England or Wales. Owen is also my father's middle name and my son's first name.

I've traced the family back to Edward Owen, 1705-1769, Halifax, Virginia. He was married to a woman from Wales, Anna Barnett. At least that is what I've been able to find. My search for Owen stops here, as there are over one million people researching "Edward Owen." I may never know the details of the family's immigration to the Colonies. I may just have to imagine them.

And I have not searched for Nancy Jane Thomasson Owen's family history—only Robert's. After all, history is made by men. After all, it is, as my mother said, "a man's world."

***

ALL OF THOSE YEARS of growing up around my mother's stepmother and brothers and sisters, all of the times Mom said something about Aunt Pearl or Grandpa Russell, I never registered what the "other part" of the family was about—who they were, how they were related. Perhaps that is why I hold so tightly to my birth name. Even though it contains two family names given by men and only one given name, I treasure it.

I will continue to fight to have my whole name acknowledged. And yes, I painted Nancy's trunk when I carried my son.

A Family Name

*Her trunk smells of another time
one hundred years ago.
Civil War.*

*Locks stick. I force them open,
break a fingernail. Rust clings
to metal spotted with old paint
and varnish, once shining golden,
like brass.*

Big with child, I dust inside,
pull yellowed paper lining, thin
as onion skin, tossed aside easy,
like a breath.

Next, cloth to line it, calico print
red, white, black, not the colors
of Confederacy, or Union. I staple,
glue cloth to rounded top, flattened
sides. Wait to dry.
I clean the outer surface, rigid,
uneven from time and wear.

Her fingers touched, pulled, packed
dresses, hats, baby shoes, maybe
even Grandmama Steve's booties, knit from
soft pink thread, ribbon woven
through to tie her feet, tiny toes
still curled from lying inside her mother.

Time to paint. I choose black,
a shiny paint to smooth
roughened sides, bring metal
locks forward for the eye,
seal wooden bands, bowed over
top, soft now like sanded wood.

I never knew her, Nancy Owen.
She never knew me, nor the son
I would bear, named for her.

I sit up straight to view my labor,
My back aches and my legs stiffen.
Straining, I carry the baby tucked
inside me, like a gift.

CHAPTER THIRTEEN

Teacher

SUMMER 2013. For the last two nights, I've dreamed about my mother.

The first night.

"She is dying," the nurse on the phone says. "She only has a few days. Come quickly."

"Can we get hospice?" I ask.

"Yes, but you still need to be here soon."

I wrestle with the logistics. I have final exams to give and read, grades to figure out. How will I juggle all of this?

I can do it all online, but Roger will have to set up temporary Internet at my mother's little house in Alabama.

Then I see my mother crawling along the ground. She lies down.

"I'm tired. I hate to go, but I'm tired," she says.

The second night. My mother is still dying, but she's up and walking.

"Nancy, you must have been to the store. My refrigerator is full. Let's have a ham sandwich," she tells me.

She grabs two slices of ham and four pieces of bread and puts them into a plastic bag.

"She's doing better," the nurse says.

Even while dying, my mother wants me to eat. She never stops caring about me.

I think I will go to her house, sleep in a bed near her. I still have my final exams to give and grade.

Always the final exams.

***

ROGER AND I LIVED for six years in Arizona, in hopes of finding a happy home for our retirement years. I retired from my full-time position at the Michigan community college. When we arrived in Arizona, I immediately checked out possibilities to teach college. I simply could not leave it. During our years there, I taught both at a community college and a small private college.

One semester at the community college, I had problems with my students. These days, challenges with students are part of the profession, even at college level. There's a sense of entitlement on the part of many students, an expectation of a high grade despite the quality of the work.

This particular class shrank to only a few students as the semester went along. Students seemed resentful and challenged my expertise. One returning student, who had(I learned later) received an easy A for an earlier class, was angry about earning Cs in my class. There was a young man on the soccer team who slumped in his desk and pulled his cap down over his eyes. There was the deaf student who had a translator.

The older student complained to the dean about my teaching. The young man, who was bright enough, continued to stare down at his desk during class, baseball cap over his eyes, either sleeping or ignoring me entirely. The deaf student decided I was disrespectful of her because I was looking mostly at her translator when I lectured. I had no training in teaching deaf students. I'd answered the student's emails during a weekend out of town. I made suggestions about improving her writing.

Yet she complained to the associate dean. Nothing I did for her was enough.

The class imploded. The only solution, the associate dean told me, was to make the class a hybrid by learning the online Blackboard system and meeting each student individually once a week.

So I learned Blackboard from scratch in the middle of the semester. The older student was given to another instructor to mentor.

In a private conference, almost in tears, I told the associate dean, Anna, that I "didn't want to teach composition anymore." I did not understand why this was happening to me, why the students seemed to turn on me for trying to give them a good class.

I assumed that I could trust Anna to understand my frustration. Yet months later, when the literary institute I was assisting was shut down by the college (a financial decision, so they said), I asked for a class. The dean waited until I returned from a conference to speak with me. We made an appointment.

Her office is dark. She has no windows, and she only has a small, dim lamp.

I enter through the main door, which opens from the office administrator's area. I hope for a swift resolution to whatever is happening.

She closes the door. She asks me to sit down at a chair in front of her desk. She speaks first.

"How is Camila?"

Asking about my granddaughter, her voice has a strange, gravely quality today, unlike her usual speaking voice. It doesn't fit her. She is a slight woman, with fair skin and hair. She knows about my granddaughter's birth a year before. She does not have grandchildren.

"She's fine. My son is struggling with work. But you know how it is," I say, to try to connect with Anna. "We can't really tell our children what to do when they're adults."

I try to laugh, but her face does not encourage me. Something strange is going on.

She speaks again, "Why did you say you didn't want to teach composition again, and why are you now asking for a comp class?"

I pause, confused and suddenly tense. The room seems close, hot.

"I said that when I was upset. I thought you understood. I thought I could talk to a colleague about what was happening in my class."

I struggle to keep my voice light and even. I feel my neck muscles tighten.

"Why did you say you didn't want to teach composition again, and why are you now asking for a comp class?" She repeats the same words, her voice dropping more deeply into a gravel pit.

"Why do you keep asking the same thing over and over again?" I say. I try to explain yet again that I was upset when I spoke those words.

"And you said you didn't want to teach women's literature either."

"Anna, (I call her by her first name), I said that after you and I had a conversation about the particular challenges of teaching that course, about the problems you faced with chauvinism and prejudice from the students. I thought you understood that I was agreeing with you... I—"

She stops me, and then begins again.

"Why did you say..."

This is surreal. I'm in this dark, warm office with this slight woman whose voice sounds as frightening as a ghoul's.

I struggle to say something that will break this strange spell.

"I thought we were colleagues, Anna."

She stands up.

"This conversation has gone too far. We'll have to take it up another time. This meeting is over."

Her office has two doors, one on either side. She moves to the door I came in and opens it. She is dismissing me.

I stand up and walk past her, leaving by the other door. I have not obeyed her. I hear a gasp.

It's been over five years since this incident happened, but the visceral feeling of being in that dark office is still real and fresh.

Searching for Nannie B.

We returned to Michigan after realizing that it would always be more like home than Arizona. I went back to my former college to teach as an adjunct, hoping to return "home" to a familiar campus. I was sure I would never have a similar experience as had occurred in Arizona.

During a winter semester, two years after returning, I received a blistering email from the associate dean. It was a response to my sharing an update about a troubled student whom I had let into my class only hours after the "never attended" deadline.

Nadia stated that "no good deed goes unpunished …

This dean had once been in another department. When her job was eliminated, and because she has a Master's degree in a related field, she moved into the English Department.

How things change.

This time, I'm only an adjunct, without job protection. Though I have a union, it can do little for me until I leave "probationary" status.

An irony of life.

What I thought was good and solid has been compromised. My body feels the poison.

At the beginning of the semester, I allowed this student into my class only hours after the "never attended" deadline because she wrote to me that unless she got into my class, she would lose her tuition money. She also told me her young daughter had died, that she could not "take anything else."

As a mother, I've often brushed away the fear and dread of this kind of loss. Two of my friends have lost their sons, one to a brain tumor and one to a car accident. How could a mother bear losing her child?

What could I do but let her enter the class?

I spent the bulk of my full-time professional years—twenty-three to be exact—at this college. These were the years I raised my son, the years of my development as a scholar, a teacher, and a mother.

These were the years of my academic success—the faculty lectureship I gave on socialism in the Frederick Manfred letters, the co-editing of the Manfred letters, along with three other books, one about the empowerment of the female voice. I worked with the Honors Program, was the Cultural Activities Coordinator and I brought in cultural programs for the college—writers, artists, lecturers.

These were also years of personal challenge. I remarried, then divorced and married Ted, a highly respected colleague, a stroke victim, after having an affair with him that became part of the public conversation.

Friends later told me that though many people disapproved of my affair with Ted, they were amazed at my efforts and my patience during my years with him, trying to help him communicate despite his aphasia. When the marriage became unworkable, we divorced. Two years later Ted took his life. I suffered a deep sadness that still returns to me in memories and dreams.

After my mother died, I moved to Arizona with my life partner, Roger. We wanted an "adventure" in a new place. As a farewell, the College president took me to lunch.

Just me.

I left this college with the vision that I had helped create something there—a cultural program, a publication to remember a beloved student who passed suddenly. I did not realize the personal impact of leaving a niche I'd created at a place that felt familiar and safe.

During our six years in Arizona, I held onto my dream of "my" college, one in which teachers were treated with respect and the faculty was unionized. I remembered it as a community of supportive teachers who worked together and treated one another with respect. When I dreamed of it, I always had an ache of longing in my chest for what I had left behind.

When we returned to Michigan and I went back to "my" college, I believed I was coming home. The full-time union president introduced me as "Emeritus Faculty."

Searching for Nannie B.

When I let the troubled student into my class, I wasn't expecting the strong response from my "boss."

"I'm sorry," I said to Nadia as she screamed at me on the phone. I felt as if I'd failed.

"Don't apologize to me. Apologize to yourself. You're the one who will have to deal with this student on your own. I want nothing to do with it. I don't want to know anything about it."

Thus began a long semester of dealing with this student's manipulative behavior, working with the Counseling Department and the Dean of Students. Near the end of the term, I wrote an email to the counselor to summarize what had transpired. I cc'd this to Nadia. That was my next mistake.

Now this angry, unpleasant email saying that I had given the other students an impression of favoritism to this student. I was an ineffective teacher. She didn't have to use the words. The idea was there.

An ineffective teacher, despite the letter I received from former students about how their lives were changed by working with me, despite the nominations for *Who's Who Among American Teachers*. A phone call to Nadia did not ease the tension. With the charm of a drill sergeant, she told me that she hoped I would "follow the rules" hereafter.

I realized only at this point that this was about asserting control, letting me know that I had no ground at all to stand on. All my years of teaching, scholarship, all the years of gaining confidence and respect meant nothing to her.

I wonder if my mother felt powerless when she was forced to retire from teaching after one year.

At least when Nannie B. Chandler left her job, she went with the accolades of students and faculty. As I've looked through my mother's files and records over the last year, I find notes after note from grateful young people who studied with her. She had tutored lawyers and writers who have earned national attention. One of them is William Bradford Huie, author of *The Revolt of Mamie*

Stover and *The Execution of Private Slovik*. He was a hometown boy, and my mother taught him Latin. Another writer, Byron Huggins, dedicated his first book to "Aunt Bee," as her young friends knew her.

I remember my mother becoming quiet in the face of disappointment or hurt. I often did not know the cause, but one occasion I do remember is when one of her oldest friends attacked her verbally while dropping her off after choir practice. This "friend" was threatened by my mother's popularity.

Was this similar to my situation with Nadia? This friend of my mother's had been connected to our family for decades. Mom had even given her some hair combs of her stepmother's, Big Mama.

That night, this woman told my mother, "You think you're so smart. Just because everybody likes you, doesn't mean you're that important."

A backlash, I believe, from jealousy of my mother because of her many friends, because of how they valued her. That night, my mother got out of the car and went into her house without saying anything. For days, I recall that she was quiet, as if wrestling with the hurt, not sharing it. I imagine it was like all the years of her silence about so many things—about my dad's troubles with drink, about her loss of friends as the military uprooted their lives again and again.

And about the hole that her mother's absence left in her life.

And now I dream of my mother, tired and dying, and yet she wants to feed me a ham sandwich.

There was always this resilience about my mother. She recovered after many dark periods. The least I can do for her is to try to restore my grandmother, Nannie B. Russell Chandler.

I seek to fill that hole in my mother's life, for her, for myself, and for my bloodline.

When I visited the grave of Nannie B. Russell Chandler, I sat beside her and talked to her. I sat under a big oak tree in the historical Bethel Church Cemetery, near graves decorated with Confederate flags. I spoke to Nannie B. Russell Chandler and told her about her wonderful daughter, about how much she longed for her mother, but what a fine woman she was. I want to bring my grandmother, and my mother and myself, out of obscurity. I want to understand how Grandmother Nannie B's absence, her erasure, from her daughter's life has affected not only my mother, but me.

Dad used to say, "You can always tell a teacher. But you can't tell her much."

As humorous as the statement is, the truth within it suggests there are certain people who are born to be teachers.

My mother was among an increasing number of women in college in the early twentieth century. I read recently that by 1920, 47.5 percent of college graduates were women. While this percentage is less than our current figure of more than 60 percent, the 1920 figure is a much larger number than I might have thought for a time when a woman's primary work was in the home.

During her one official teaching year, 1927-1928, my mother wrote a piece that she presented to the Thursday Afternoon Club in Hartselle. Her name at the top of the first page reads "Bee Chandler," yet another of her signatures. She writes of her discouragement at realizing that though she had graduated with the credentials to teach, she still faced the reality that "ambition and knowledge were not sufficient in themselves." She says she was "defeated even before I started to teach."

The resilience she would show in later stages of her life helped her to nurture her dream. She writes, "I learned quickly that I must meet the challenges necessary to accomplish my purpose. I was determined to be a teacher; and to be a teacher with experience, I had to make a start toward getting this experience. From then on, teaching was a wonderful adventure for me." When Nannie B. Chandler wrote these words, she had not yet married, and perhaps she had not even met my father. She did not know that she would in a teaching position for only one year. This would not deter her from being a teacher all of her life. While raising her children, she continued to study Latin and French, and until she left Alabama for Michigan in the early 1990s, she substituted at the high school and tutored young people, men and women, in grammar and French.

She studied poetry with her friend, Kitty—they read Wordsworth, Emily Dickinson, Ann Sexton. I have her books, both the college Latin books and her later ones—a copy of *Using Latin*, the text I also studied in high school Latin classes. Her copy is frayed on the edges of the cover, filled with notes throughout the pages. She continued to write poetry and maintained her membership in the Alabama Poetry Society.

A teacher's teacher. I am my mother's daughter. As much as I didn't want to be like her when I was a teenager, as embarrassed as I was that she was so much older than my friends' mothers, as much as I wanted to distinguish myself from her during young adulthood, I always went back to our common ground—languages, literature, and teaching.

Mom always wanted to know about my studies, especially English and French. In college I decided to major in them both, partly because of her. I took a full regimen of French classes, though I never felt proficient enough to teach it.

Many years later in August 1991, Mom would write to me:

> *Now, Nancy,*
> *I come to what I'm really trying to express—my deep and [sic] appreciation for <u>YOU</u> and what you have meant in my life. <u>You light up my life and make it <u>fun</u>, challenging</u> and <u>meaningful.</u> I have enjoyed reading many things which you have suggested and always I'm to have a new challenge whether in reading a book or experimenting with a new project which you suggested.*
> *Anyway, I hope you always will know that I love you; and I feel that in many ways we are as one person in our quest of the good things that life has to offer. <u>MUSIC, LITERATURE, POETRY, ART</u> etc. etc.*

My mother imprinted me.

What would it have been like for me *not* to have my mother? Not to know her, or anything about her? What if I believed I had caused her death? How much more pain, grief, and guilt, would my life have held? How would I have turned out without her presence—the music, the poetry and literature, all of the ways of thinking she passed on to me?

I cannot let these two women, or anyone else, for that matter, bring me into oblivion. Like my mother, I will continue to teach and learn, even when I no longer enter a classroom of students. I will stay "above ground," visible and open to new ideas.

I will not be buried, like my grandmother, Nannie B. Russell Chandler, without a story.

CHAPTER FOURTEEN
Birthday

MADIGAN HOSPITAL, Fort Lewis, Washington, ca. June 15, 1946.

To Betty and Marjorie:

Hello girls,

How are you both feeling today? I hear you kept late hours last night. But you had a chance to rest today so all's O.K.

I'm feeling alright even if I did stay awake all last night,

The flowers are really beautiful. I'll enjoy them lots—thanks so much for them.

You will have to manage someway about your clothes—keep you underwear and socks washed out and your dresses hung up.

Nancy is fine today. She is taking almost 2 oz. of milk at a feeding. In fact, she is just a little piggish, anyway! By the time she comes home I think she will be real pretty _ like your daddy. She doesn't resemble me any. like your Betty, your daddy says you aren't eating much. You must eat so you will get to feeling well and you can't do good work without food.

Marjorie, how are you doing? Don't eat too many banana splits. Guess this is hard to read but I'm flat on my back.

Be good and take care of your daddy for me.

Mother

I sure miss you 3.

In my life, birthdays have always been significant. My mother and my sister Marge always did things to make them special, a kind of sacrament, a remembering. On Mom's birthday, July 12, she never mentioned the details of her birth, even after I knew about my grandmother's untimely death. Only when she defended her name did she talk about her mother's premature death.

But my birthday was special. My sisters had left home by the time I was eleven, so the attention was on me on June 14, every year. Mom usually talked about what a surprise I had been, coming to her when she was forty. There was the year my father arranged a skywriting of my name as a surprise. There were birthday parties for me wherever we lived, on a base in Oklahoma, in a town in Texas, anywhere. At our last military assignment in Sault Ste. Marie, Michigan, my best friend Carla and I celebrated together. Her birthday was only days after mine.

Decades after Carla and I parted at the end of the eighth grade, we found one another through social media. She sent me a photo of that party. We wore matching plaid shorts outfits.

"It's the only birthday party I ever had," Carla told me on the phone before sending me the photo.

How strange that seems to me, to have only one birthday party during one's childhood.

I've carried that feeling of sacrament into my adult life. Sometimes significant birthdays of people in my life have coincided with other dates to create what feels like a cosmic pattern. My previous husband, Ted's, birthday was on March 12, the date of my father's death. Ted committed suicide just before March 12, when he was to turn sixty-five. March 16 was the date of my parent's wedding. When Dad died, they were four days short of celebrating forty years.

March is often a sad month of memories for me.

My father's birthday is December 14. Of course, he often quipped that he had married an "older woman" because my mother's birthday was July 12 of the previous year. With the idea of celebrating Dad's life, I married my life partner Roger on December 14, 1996. Mom was present in her green velvet pantsuit, still thriving at ninety years old. It was a blessed day.

Only days after my birth, Mom wrote my sisters and Dad a letter from the hospital. It's written in pencil, and she says she is "flat on her back." This was a time when women stayed in the hospital for a few days to recover after childbirth. I must also remember that, at the time of my birth, a woman's having a baby at forty years old was considered dangerous to both the woman and the child.

Mom writes about me that "by the time she comes home I think she will be real pretty—like your daddy. She doesn't resemble me any."

Yet Nannie B Chandler was considered quite a catch. In her college scrapbook, she pasted a business card of Allen A. Simpson. Beneath it is a note written on the back of another card:

> To whom it may concern, know ye that… Nannie B. Chandler has, this 28th day of April, Nineteen hundred and twenty-five, faithfully promised to be true unto me until death doth us part.
> Allen A. Simpson
> Duly sworn & verified before me this day. April 25, 1928. [unreadable signature]

Even though there were men who wanted to date her in college, Mom did not believe in her own beauty.

Does this have anything to do with the circumstances of her birth or with her mother's untimely death? Was this her lifelong birthday present, this feeling of inadequacy, this sense of not ever being enough?

It is mine as well, a legacy of never being or doing enough, of never stopping to produce, to give, in order to feel that I'm not wasting my time on the planet. It's *my original sin*, the heavy coat of my childhood.

***

A STUDENT RECENTLY POSTED an article on my Facebook page about DNA and ancestral issues. It's about epigenetics, the scientific theory that there are methyl groups that attach themselves to DNA and pass along imprints of life events such as trauma or joy, to following generations. This suggests to me that a grandmother's issues in life could be passed down to her granddaughter.

I've read the article four times now, looked up epigenetic research on the web, and spoken with my counselor about the issue. If this is true, I could be carrying not only Nannie B. Russell Chandler's musical gene, but also traumatic events that happened to her and to my mother.

I picture again the bedroom on July 12, 1905, where Nannie B. is struggling to have her baby, her tall husband Robert pacing back and forth. I see her skin glistening with sweat and hear her moans, the doctor's voice, "Push, push, Nannie B." I see the baby come out, slippery and crying, the mother hold her, then fall asleep. She will never awaken. The father will weep. He will give the baby to Nannie B.'s sister Mary, who will take her home and raise her with her other children as if she were hers.

I hear again my cousin Helen's voice on the phone, describing my mother in 1908 as a small girl of three, pulled from her Aunt Mary's arms by Nannie Dixie Robinson Chandler, or perhaps by the girl's father, Robert Chandler.

Had my mother even seen her father during those three years, other than the day Robert Chandler had a photo made with his first child, a baby girl? Did she even know he was her father?

Helen says that the little girl did not want to leave, that she reached her arms out to her aunt, that she begged to stay with the only mother she had known. Helen says that the girl cried.

Helen continues. Aunt Mary Humphrey, who was Helen's grandmother, "just about died" when they took little Bee away.

Mary did die two years later, in 1910, after little Nannie B was taken from her household. One daughter, Pearl, who was thirteen, went to live with her grandfather (my great-grandfather) John R. Russell and his new wife Clemanzie. Delilah Jane, my great grandmother, had died in 1905, the same year as her daughter Nannie B. And Emma B., another of Aunt Mary's daughters, went to live with Grandfather Chandler, or "Uncle Ed," as Helen called him, and his new wife, Nannie Dixie Robinson Chandler.

Emma B. was sixteen. The 1910 U. S. census lists her relationship with the Chandler family as "none." *From the Chandler and Russell household, a baby girl is born. The mother dies, and the baby lives with the Russell Aunt until the Chandler father brings a new mother, a Robinson woman. After the Russell aunt dies two years later, one of her daughters goes to live in the Chandler and Robinson household.*

Is this what is called coming "full circle"?

What traumas were passed from mother to newborn baby on July 12, 1905? The small baby girl who had just left the comfort and wet warmth of her mother's womb, what did she feel when she could not return to the familiar scent of her mother's body, to a warmth that would have helped her make the difficult transition into the outside world?

And then three years, until 1908, with a family, other children. A home, she must have thought. A safe place.

Bee was taken away some time after April 19, 1908 by her daddy and a new Mama Chandler, a young woman, merely eighteen years old, who had just married this tall, handsome businessman of thirty-three. From that day on, my mother would feel somehow "different" from the others. How confusing it must have been. She probably did not remember the trauma of birth, her mother's death or the pain of being pulled from her arms, but she may have carried it, along with the grief of her father and her aunts, who must have wept when Nannie B. Russell Chandler died.

As I write this, I want to curl up in a fetal position under a blanket and hide. To return to a time before I existed. I want to erase myself. I want to shut out the grey, dismal sky I see from my study window. Close the curtain on branches, one or two lone leaves still holding on this chilly fall morning, a border of my view of a golf course across the street. Leaves on bare branches mock me with their hanging on.

So many times my mother sat at the table, a cup of coffee cooling in her hand, and said she thought that gloomy days like this were sad. That she felt lonely, even depressed. On Sundays, in particular, after the flurry of Sunday school, church, and perhaps a lunch out with relatives, there was a lull, a silence. I joined her in feeling this silence, almost like a grave. We were supposed to be holy, or to be praying, I guess. It never worked for me or for my mother.

Most of the time my parents did nothing on Sunday afternoons except read the paper, and perhaps my dad would watch television, maybe a baseball game.

Before the silence, there were Sunday afternoons at Papa and Mama Steve Nelson's. We went to their house to sit and visit on the front porch on warm days, inside on cooler days. The men of the family, Uncle Skinny, Uncle Willard, along with my Dad, would gather in the next room in a cluster that looked like a football team sharing the next game play. They would tell jokes they thought unsuited for "polite company." I never heard what they said, just the burst of laughter that came from the cluster after the punch line … my dad's cigarette smoke spiraling above his head as he coughed and laughed, his face flushed with the effort.

After Mama and Papa Steve died, and then my father, those Sundays were empty. Quiet as a tomb.

Even now, in the midst of my life of writing and teaching, my work at First Unitarian Universalist Church of Detroit, I find myself awash with darkness. My understanding of myself is skewed by a sense of shame and inadequacy, a feeling of failure, that I am not good enough, loving enough, productive enough. That I'm taking up space on the planet that could be better occupied by a more deserving and capable person. I want praise and attention. Then when I get it, I'm uncomfortable, as if I'm not worth any except negative attention, and criticism.

Yet last Sunday, our minister, Reverend Mohr, talked about the importance of hearing the "cosmic drum." We are inseparable from the cosmos, so that when we act and live, we should live in harmony with it.

How? I've had so many times in my life when, moving along at a good clip, I find myself tripped up with emotions that seem to have no origin. They come to me in an instant. Perhaps it's a sound of a siren, or the scent of roses, or carnations (my mother's idea of a "funeral flower"), or perhaps magnolias, which evokes afternoons on Big Mama's porch. Or it can be a Philip Sousa march on the radio. I feel my throat close, tears forming in my eyes. I'm suddenly standing on a side of the parade field at Ladd Air Force Base in Alaska, or on the sidewalk in any of the towns we lived in in Texas or Oklahoma. I see Dad's straight back, his body moving with the beat of the march, the growled command he gives to his battalion as they march by.

This darkness can come to me at any time, without warning. It's usually associated with scents, or sounds, the powerful threads that draw me back into my past.

Is this the manifestation of my mother's dislocation and alienation? Am I like the little girl who overheard the women say that she should be dead and her mother alive?

***

MY MOTHER'S DEATH on October 23, 2001, brought her life full circle, back to July 12, 1905. As she was born, she died. I've heard it said that dying is akin to childbirth. The effort to leave life and the effort to enter life are both labors. In my letter to my mother after her death, I describe her gasping in the last minutes, as a mother gasps to push out her baby. She said over and over that she wanted to "go to bed." As it turns out, she was also saying "up there," pointing to a space above our heads where I could see nothing. My husband Roger heard her say it. I did not. He told me as we lay in bed after her death, trying to go to sleep.

I hope she was seeing her mother for the first time in ninety-six years.

***

IN THE LETTER to my mother I also wrote, "You gave me my history. I was born from you. Now you have gone and, in an important way, you have reentered me, growing inside in a new kind of life that is free of pain and fatigue and discouragement."

Perhaps the discouragement, the moments of darkness, have been passed down through two generations of loss and grief.

In bringing Nannie B. Russell Chandler into the light, perhaps I can lift the darkness that I inherited from both Nannie B.s.

Nancy Owen Nelson

The New Stone Placed with Original Grave Marker

CHAPTER FIFTEEN
A New Stone

IN JULY 2013, my husband and I drive to Alabama to find out more about my family. On our first day, we visit Mom's and Dad's graves.

The flowers I hung on a hook above the graves the year before are still in place, purples and yellows faded by the sun. With scissors, we clip back the grass from the flat headstones. The plan is to squirt them with cleaner and water from plastic bottles and scrub them both with a brush.

First Roger cleans Dad's military-issue stone, a bronze piece that lies close to the ground.

"Brush from the center outward, like this," Roger says as he works. "It will move the mud off of the stone."

Once he finishes, I can see the gray metal lettering, much clearer than when I visited last June. The brass background glimmers. The stone looks almost as it did when it was laid forty-five years ago.

There is a cross at the top, center. Then the inscription:

WOODFORD O NELSON ALABAMA
LT COL U S ARMY WORLD WAR II
DEC 14 1905 – MARCH 12 1968

Searching for Nannie B.

As I recall, it was easy for Mom to order the gravestone. She just contacted the Army and they sent the stone, a standard, military issue. Decades later, I would think and think again about what to put on my mother's stone.

When Roger finishes with the brush, I kneel on the grass and work on Mom's stone. The brass-colored flowers around the edge stand out now. They glisten in the hot Alabama sunlight at midday. The metallic center shines so that the writing is clear. After her name, and birth and death dates, is the engraving of the last two lines of a poem she wrote to Dad only weeks after his death in 1968.

"Reflections"
Eventide will come at last,
But our love will never die.

When I ordered this stone after she died in 2001, I looked for the right words to say who she was and what she valued. She told me near the end of her life that for all of those years, she still talked to Dad in her moments of trial and loss. She loved him and he was her husband forever. The poem says it all.

Today I realize that I left her maiden name, *Chandler*, off of the stone. It's ironic, since I'm so obsessed with names. Why would I omit the name of the father who gave his seed, who brought her home to a new mother when she was three? A father who gave her a piano when she was ten or eleven, telling her, "You have a special gift. Don't ever refuse to play if anyone asks." A father who, when he heard her play, looked on with tears in his eyes and said in a voice full of tears, "You remind me of your mother." At the time of my mother's death, I did not realize fully that Robert Chandler allowed his beloved first wife, Nannie B. Russell Chandler, to become a shadowy figure, that he had a stone made for her that says only her name, misspelled, and the words "wife of R. E. Chandler." I did not know then what I was told years later by Helen, that "Big Auntie," Nannie Dixie Robinson, was jealous of Robert's first wife. I did not

124

know that he allowed her to keep information from my mother all of those years.

There is no doubt her mother's absence and this silence about her shaped Nannie B.'s life. What a difference it would have made if Robert Chandler and his new wife had been open with my mother, had answered her questions in a loving way.

But still, why did I leave off the *Chandler* from the gravestone?

I remember Mom mentioning off and on through the years that no one talked about her mother, but she didn't seem to know why. Now I understand that her unease in the family had to do with Big Mama's jealousy and unwillingness to offer information. My mother told me from time to time that she did not feel connected to her half-siblings, that she felt like an outsider. Maybe I subconsciously chose to identify her only with her mother and her husband. Maybe I'm angry at my grandfather for not keeping his first wife's memory alive for her daughter.

After leaving the Hartselle graveyard, Roger and I drive to the New Hope, Bethel Cemetery, where my grandmother and other Russell ancestors are buried. As I did the summer before when I was alone, we drive through winding, two-lane roads, trees and green growth flourishing on either side of the road.

I ask aloud, "What must it have been like to live here one hundred years ago? They only had wagons. Everyone farmed."

We talk about it for a few minutes, both of us in awe of the ability of these tough Scots-Irish people to exist on their own. Their work, their families, and their churches kept them going. Roger should know. In his youth, he lived for a while on a relative's farm, working the land, caring for the horses and cows.

In my ancestral research of my grandmother, I've seen that many women died in childbirth. This is evident when I find a family with fourteen children on a census, ten of whom were birthed by a first wife and four by a second.

Nannie B. Russell Chandler had only one child.

Searching for Nannie B.

This is why I knew when I came home from Alabama last year that we had to place a new stone. And that is where we are driving today, to see the stone.

Last winter I was going through some financial files and I saw a notice of a $1000 CD with a Hartselle bank. I was co-signer.

I recalled that I tried to find out about the CD by calling the bank, but I'd given up after several tries with a state and regional office. I put it aside for "later." *Now it's time to follow up on this,* I thought. *And I could purchase a new stone for Grandmother Chandler. Or rather, Mom can purchase a stone for her mother from money she put aside years ago.*

I called the Hartselle, Alabama, branch of the bank and talked with a woman who looked up records on the account.

"Goodness, this has been a long time," she said in a soft southern voice, emphasizing the vowels. "I'll need proof of your relationship to Nannie B. Nelson. And I'll need a death certificate."

I told her that I would send an official copy of the certificate and a Xerox of my driver's license.

Mom died in a Livonia, Michigan, hospital near her care facility. After making some calls, I found that I would need to go to the Livonia City Hall to get the certificate.

When I picked it up from the clerk, a feeling of dissociation came over me. I glanced over the form. It contained blanks that had been filled in with basic information—name, date of birth, date and place of death, cause of death—*acute ischemic bowel*, a condition my mother had suffered for years, even having surgery in her mid-eighties. But why was there a choice for years of education? "College was checked, with the number 4 following.

What difference did it make whether she finished high school or attended college?

Regardless of how educated she was, my mother was gone.

I sent the death certificate and my driver's license to the bank employee. She needed a few days, she said, and she would mail me a check for the CD.

That was at the end of 2012.

I would soon order a new stone for Nannie B. Russell Chandler.

During my trip alone last summer, I made a quick visit to the Madison County Historical Records in Huntsville. I found and touched Robert Chandler and Nannie B. Russell's marriage certificate, as well as a subsequent marriage certificate of my great grandfather, John R. Russell, to his second wife Clemenzie. As with the Bethel Church records with Grandpa Russell's writing, I felt a certain surge of warmth in my fingers. These documents had actually been touched by my ancestors.

I've always thought that viewing official documents related to people I've known and loved would seem sterile. The essence of a person isn't represented on official papers. No flesh and blood, no sense of the person's energy, her life, her passions. Not so with my Huntsville visit, nor with last summer's visit to the Morgan County Archives in Decatur.

The archival collection is located just down the street from my grandfather's—Robert Chandler's—store on Second Avenue. I spend four hours in an afternoon going through folders labeled for three of my family lines: Owen, Nelson, and Chandler. I have already researched the Russells the summer before in the Madison County records.

I expect these documents to be sterile like my mother's death certificate.

While looking through a file folder listed "Nelson," my heart jumps when I find two news articles about *Mrs. W. O. Nelson*. One reports that after my father's death in 1968, my mother increased her work with young people, in particular students who wanted to be tutored in English grammar, Latin, or French. She made lasting friendships among them, and the articles in the *Hartselle Enquirer* stated just that—"Nelson has Tutored Generations of Hartselle's Young People," and "Tutoring the Young Keeps Woman, 86, Busy as a Bee." (My mother's nickname "Bee" had always been associated with the insect, a kind of "helper.")

As I sit at a table in the chilly archive office, I am proud of Nannie B. Chandler Nelson, a woman who did not let the instability of military life negate her life, nor let it be negated by her husband's death, or by her increasing age. She was productive even at the end of her life—writing poetry in her head and dictating to me or her music therapist, plunking away at the piano, which she had in her room at her last residence. She maintained her creativity until her death at ninety-six.

If only Nannie B. Russell Chandler could have known the child she birthed.

Among the legal documents in the archives, I find my Nelson grandparents' and my parents' marriage licenses; great-grandfather Robert Goodman Owen's will with S. M. Nelson (my grandfather) as executor, and step-grandmother Nannie Dixie Robinson Chandler's will with signed pages from all of the children, including my mother. I find them by looking into an index under their names. The documents are pristine, bound in a big volume and organized by date. Unlike Mom's death certificate, they are documents of the living. The hands of my family touched them and signed them. Mom's signature on her stepmother's will is familiar. I immediately recognize Dad's signature on the marriage license in 1928; it's the same as it was on his military documents later in his life. I find the marriage license of my Nelson grandparents. They were married in 1901. As I did when I touch Robert and Nannie B.'s marriage certificate, I marvel that these are the original documents that my kin read and signed.

As I read over Nannie Dixie Chandler's will, I note that all of her children, Robert, Norma, Ruth, and David, as well my mother, signed papers agreeing to the will's probation. I read these lines:

> *I do hereby will, devise and bequeath all of my estate including real, personal and mixed property and money... and all property rights of every sort, kind and description wherever located, which I may own or to which I may [be] entitled to at the time of my death, to Nannie B. Nelson... "in equal portion, share and share alike.*

In equal portion, share and share alike. Big Mama *did* try to love
my mother as her own child.

In mid-afternoon on our first day in Alabama, Roger and I drive
to see the new stone. We arrive in New Hope, the community I visited
the summer before to meet Priscilla Scott, the genealogist. Priscilla
has promised to lead us to the Old Bethel Cemetery. As Priscilla
and I did last year, we pick up John Ed Butler, the proprietor of the
cemetery. He shows us briefly around the house. He has refinished
the church pew from Old Bethel Church, which my grandmother
attended, and it sits in front of a window in the kitchen. The dark
wood glimmers in the sunlight; a soft green cushion covers the
seating area. At the end is a copy of *National Geographic Magazine.*

Back on the road, John Ed in the car with Priscilla, and we drive
one or two miles down the winding Madison County roads toward
the graveyard.

This is real farm country, I note. No GPS coverage. The two-
lane roads meander past farms with fields of corn or wheat, recently
sowed. We pass grazing cows and horses. The most frequent sights are
churches—usually every mile or so, usually Baptist. We pass Poplar
Ridge Community School, the one-room schoolhouse Nannie B.
Russell, her sisters, and Lucy Butler attended. Again, I imagine her
walking to school or riding in the back of a wagon with her three
sisters, her father driving the horses.

We pass the Old Bethel Church, where I was welcomed last
year to a Sunday night service in the middle of a rainstorm. I think
of Syrethia, the elder's wife, who has multiple sclerosis. I remember
the singing and the preaching. I remember the people's kindness, a
simple grace—the handshaking and blessings, the prayers for the
sick, the prayer I offered for Nannie B. Russell Chandler.

A half-mile further, we turn left on Keel Hollow Road. The
cemetery is a short distance after the turn. It looks just the same as
when I visited last year.

The four of us walk among the gravestones. I head immediately
toward the back, where my grandmother lies. Roger follows me. As

I get closer, I see that the blue and purple flowers I purchased at Walmart are still in front of the stone. They are faded but still there, and they give grace to the stone's bareness.

Somehow, this is a comfort.

Turning to my right, I look toward the foot of the grave to see the new stone, grey granite, with double-lined framing around the words in the center:

NANNIE B. RUSSELL CHANDLER
JULY 1879 – JULY 05, 1905
Beloved Wife of Robert Edward Chandler
Beloved Mother of Nannie B. Chandler

Roger, Priscilla and John Ed move away, looking at other graves. They know I want time alone with my grandmother. I sit down next to the grave. A chipmunk has dug a hole midway between the head and foot.

I speak to Nannie B. Russell Chandler:

"Now you are complete. Your information is all here—your husband's name, your daughter's name, and the fact that they loved you."

I want to hear her speaking to me. I want to know she understands. But there is only silence.

When ordering the stone, my sister Betty and I discussed the language on the stone. When I suggested "beloved mother," Betty paused a minute and then said, "But Mom didn't know her mother." "Good point. But she loved her nonetheless. She loved the little she knew about her."

"You're right."

So here it is, proof to the world that Nannie B. Russell Chandler's memory is not forgotten. She had a husband who loved her, who for whatever reasons could not bring himself to finish her stone or to talk to his daughter about her. She had a daughter whose life was defined by her mother's absence.

This must be my mother's restless longing, the creeping darkness that would appear on an idle Sunday afternoon or after visits with her half-siblings. It must have been an inherited loss, the trauma of both the dying mother and the baby she bore.

It is my aching loss as well.

Roger, John Ed and Priscilla moved toward grandmother's grave. It's time to leave again.

I marvel at my joy, my luck in life. I have a kind and loving husband, one who lets me be myself, who accepts me with my birth name, my independence, my restlessness, my search.

My sense of loss recedes.

CHAPTER SIXTEEN
Endurance

IN AUGUST, after returning to Michigan, I browse through bags and boxes of family records, unpacking and sorting letters, cards, and other family memorabilia into piles and boxes. I sit on the floor of my study for hours, classical piano music in the background and, as in a time warp, travel back to my birth, to the congratulatory cards my mother saved in a scrapbook, and to a letter from my Fairbanks, Alaska, kindergarten teacher, who wrote us after we returned to the continental United States.

Some days I weep as I read my mother's letters—moments of joy and excitement, days busy with reading and studying poetry with her neighbor, Kitty. I revisit the zenith moments of my life that she salvaged. My high school graduation program. My tapping for Mortar Board, an honorary society. My college graduation program dated June 1968—three months after Dad's death while my first husband, Ben, was in a tuberculosis sanatorium. News articles. My PhD. I think back on how much I've been through with all of my marriages and divorces, my miscarriage at age twenty-three. I remember that my mother was always there for me.

I find a letter for an older friend, Mary Jane, who apparently wrote to me after one of my visits. This was probably during the 1970s. She writes: "Your journey will include all the passions, defeats, radiance, ambiguities that any woman can encompass. Perhaps your experience of life as an undaunted and fearless seeker will make a fine novel someday."

Mary Jane's words could easily be said about my mother, Nannie B. Chandler Nelson. She lived her life, maintaining the passion for exploration and learning. She was an "undaunted and fearless seeker."

And my mother never deserted me when my life decisions could have caused an irreparable rift between us. When I lost a baby after my affair with the professor, she asked me to come home, but only if I wanted to. She never made me feel guilty or stained.

For each of my marriages, my mother expressed anger only one time—when she felt that I had been devalued. On the other end of the telephone, her voice was tight.

"Don't ever do this again, Nancy. Don't ever let anyone treat you this way again."

She believed in dignity, for herself and for me.

My mother wrote many letters to her daughters during her lifetime. Always she told of what she was doing and asked about us or responded to what she knew about each of our lives.

As I sit on my study floor going through and sorting papers, I hear her voice in my head. In a letter written on my parents' wedding anniversary, March 16, 1986, she wrote

Dear Nancy,

Hope all is better for you by now. On this "special" day of remembering (for me) I'm enumerating many of the good things that have happened to me.

And certainly, I am thinking of the people who have made me happy. My daughters are at the top of this list!

Nancy, you have given me the inspiration to keep on, no matter what—to keep the flame of LEARNING ablaze! Thank you for this, and for all you have meant to me. And for all our continued understanding and acceptance of each other through all these years. The "threads of circumstances" only make our understanding of each other more strong!

I love you, Mom

Searching for Nannie B.

After Mom's death, her friend Kitty told me, "Nancy, you were the love of her life." I inhaled quickly when I heard these words. I'd never viewed our relationship this way. I always thought the love of her life was Woodford Owen Nelson.

Nannie B. Chandler Nelson writes on May 12, 1974, after receiving roses from me, probably for Mother's Day (apparently I was having a difficult time with friends):

> *Dear Nancy,*
>
> *Before I get into the details of this letter, I want to thank you again for the beautiful red roses. Nancy, they are perfect and I've already enjoyed them so much. It's a real treat for me and very thoughtful of you to send them …the gesture of your sending them will last on and on. I have been so "blue" lately, I really needed the excitement of receiving flowers. Again, Nancy, my thanks for this special gift. You are special to me.*
>
> *Now I wish I could help you by sending you the answer to all your problems…. there's so little that I can do. I don't have to remind you that I'm here to help in any way that I can. Life gets so complicated for me too, of course in a different way. No males want me and I must confess I'm not anxious to be involved with them. Even at my age [69], I had the opportunity but passed it up. I think I'm glad I did. Of course, we never know about "the road not taken." I do know that my freedom is worth more than the fringe (?) benefits I could have received if I had snatched at the opportunities I could have had.*

No males want me? She once told me about one man who was fixing her toilet. When she went in to observe his work, he pressed her against the wall, making suggestive comments. She told me that she pushed him away from her. After that, she stayed clear of him. Report him? Not in this small town. It would become the gossip of the day. Another man she knew stopped her in the grocery store in

134

the meat section. He invited her to his house that night to eat the steaks he was buying. She told him no, politely.

Fringe benefits I could have received? After my father's death, Mom applied for her widow's pension. Certainly, she would have one after her husband's thirty years of military service. She was told that there was no pension. Apparently, my father had failed to sign up at the appropriate time.

She found this out at Redstone Arsenal in Huntsville, Alabama; Betty and her husband had driven her there to make her application. On the way back, instead of responding in fear or anger, she looked out of the window and commented on a light snow that had fallen.

"Isn't it beautiful?" she said.

When word got out that Owen Nelson had left his wife no pension, one of the town gossips whispered, "Owen drank up all of his money." Angry, I wanted to confront her, to tell her to shut up, or something worse.

I was fighting for my father *and* for my mother.

As it turned out, one of my friends was a Kappa Alpha man from Dad's chapter at Birmingham-Southern. He was able to go through the bureaucracy to get Mom a pension under "service-connected disability," related to a stomach ulcer he had suffered in New Guinea during World War II.

Yes, if I think about it, my mother endured much in her lifetime. She made proverbial lemonade from her challenges when she tutored young people for free, and when she led the children's choir at her church; when she helped edit a book, *Our Many Selves*, with several church women.

She did just fine without another man in her life.

CHAPTER SEVENTEEN
Another Stone

IT'S NOVEMBER, and the approach of the holidays. The Michigan weather has turned cool, with occasional warmer days to remind us of climate change. I've worried for years about global warming, about the failure of some factions in our country to acknowledge that humans are impacting the climate. Some students in my class complain about the cold, even though we haven't hit freezing temperatures.

"Think about what it would mean if we had warm weather all the time. The planet would be on the way to disaster," I remind one student as we walk to the library for an orientation, the leaves drifting from the sky to the ground.

"That's true," she says.

How many of the younger people think about their responsibility to the planet? Most of them see and experience only what is around them. *Solipsism*, as our minister talked about recently, *the world is only about me.*

Mostly I worry about future decades when my son and my granddaughter will face even more extreme effects of the earth's warming.

I won't be here with them, but I still worry.

But perhaps I will be with them as my mother is with me, and as her mother, Nannie B. Russell Chandler, was with her even though she had little information about her.

In this effort to find and acknowledge the existence of my grandmother, I want to be remembered, not erased, when I leave.

December 2013. I'm reviewing the pictures from our June trip to Alabama. I want to admire the gravestone we purchased with Mom's CD money.

I look closely at the stone, where I sat and talked to Grandmother Chandler last summer and lay on the ground next to her grave, the distant hum of cicadas and bird calls as they rustled in the trees. The ground was rough under my back, uneven with roots and pebbles, patches of grass.

I wanted to have a view from her grave.

In the photo, the surface of the new stone is smooth. The granite surface reflects patches of sun that escape between tree branches.

I admire the inscription on the stone. Then I see the dates: *July 1897 – July 5, 1905*

The date of death is wrong.

How could I, after all of the research, the probing, the travel … how could I give the wrong date to the stone maker? The wrong death date for my grandmother and, worst of all, the wrong birth date for my mother?

I review my emails to the monument company. Yes, I did give him the wrong date, a day of the month that is the same as the year of death / birth.

This makes no sense to me. I tend to hurry through details. Having been diagnosed recently with ADHD, I sometimes lose my focus. Is that what happened?

I call Roy at the monument company. His voice, thick with southern drawl, says "Nancy, I'm so sorry."

I tell him, "Make another stone. It's my mistake. Use the same credit card number."

He tells me that other customers have made mistakes, that one woman wanted to make this his fault or the fault of the monument makers…

"No, this is my responsibility," I tell him.

I feel like a fool. All of my bragging about this new stone, my talk to Nannie B. Russell Chandler about her daughter, and the date is wrong.

I call my sister, Betty.

"Oh… I'm so sorry," she says. She hasn't noticed the incorrect date either.

I could leave it as it is, save the money. But why would I want to leave a stone with the wrong dates after my dismay at displaying a marker with incomplete information, a misspelled name, for a hundred years? I can't do it.

I push aside the thought that Mom paid for a stone engraved with an incorrect date. I accept my error.

I move forward. We'll make a new stone.

I contact Priscilla and ask if she will take another photo when the correct stone is laid

"You could leave the one that's there now. No one will notice."

"It has to be right," I tell her, with more force in my voice than I intend.

Weeks later, Roy calls and tells me that the stone is ready to be laid.

"What do we do with the old stone? We usually just throw the stones behind the cemetery into the woods."

I ask him if he would get permission to set the incorrect stone near the grave.

I can't think about casting the flawed stone away. Even in its imperfections, it represents something. Exactly what, I'm not sure.

"I'll pick it up when I go to Alabama next."

A few days more and I call Priscilla to ask her to take a photo.

"Sure, I'll be going out in a few days."

When I receive her email, I open the photos immediately.

The photo she has sent is of the old stone. She's not realized that the new stone is in the place of the old one.

"Priscilla, could you go again? The picture you sent was of the incorrect stone."

"The monument people made a mistake, Nancy."

My chest hurts.

"Please look again, Priscilla."

She agrees to, tells me that she deleted some of the photos from the last visit. At last, another email arrives with more photos, this time, of the newer, correct stone.

The stone is different, without the shiny border of the first stone. But the dates are correct this time.

Nannie B. Nelson
about 3-4 years old

Nancy with her father,
Woodford Owen Nelson

Nannie B. Russell

Nannie B. Chandler Nelson

Nancy Owen Nelson

CHAPTER EIGHTEEN
Legacy

DURING THE SEARCH for my grandmother and for the source of my mother's pain, I have encountered the joy of discovering the humor and poignancy of family stories. I have experienced darkness and sorrow, often unattached to anything I can identify. Now I believe this drowning in a pit of despair, this ache in my body that makes me question my very existence, began in 1905 with the birth of a baby girl and the death of a young woman who was her mother. I believe it has continued with that child's, my mother's, life of uncertainty, longing, and pain, which she, like me, could not identify. In the beginning of my search, I did not see the relationship of my mysterious grandmother's life and death to my own. Now I understand the connection.

I have inherited this pain through my body as well as my soul, and have added my own losses—my lack of a stable home during my childhood, my father's untimely death at sixty-two after his lifetime of depression and sadness; my disappointment in marriage, the miscarriage of a lover's baby, another marriage fraught with anger; and yet another marriage to an addicted man, damaged by stroke, followed by his suicide two years after our divorce. Scattered among these losses were the joys of sharing my mother's final years as she lived near me in a care facility, of watching my son grow into manhood and become a father, and at last, of finding my life partner who is my best friend.

Searching for Nannie B.

For me there were many turning points in this journey.

One was finding the record of my grandmother's burial in an obscure graveyard in rural Madison County, Alabama, when I saw a photo of the rude stone with scant information about this young woman. Another, when I visited the grave and touched her stone and the stones of my other ancestors, scrubbed and decorated them after decades of neglect. My discovery of a third cousin who knew my mother and heard stories about my mother's early years—this filled me with love for my mother as a young child and as a young woman, the losses she faced as well as the joys of her friendship with Helen, their talks while lying on the bed. The moment when I held the buttons from Nannie B. Russell's clothing in my hands and felt their smoothness and energy, and especially the moment when I wound my mother's hair around the buttons reconnecting mother and daughter for the first time in over a century—her DNA to my mother's DNA, to my own.

My connection with my mother's loss and pain made sense when I learned of epigenetics and the possibility that, not only did my mother carry her mother's death in her body, but I, too, have carried it. I now see that some of that darkness I have experienced in my life is linked to this thread of inheritance.

If I run the filmstrip of my mother's life as I know it, she is first a squalling baby taken quickly from her dying mother's arms and placed into her aunt's. Three years later, she is a toddler passed again into another's arms, her stepmother's. At this moment she is crying because she does not want to leave the only home she has known. Then she is a young girl raised in a home with half-siblings, not understanding why she always feels set apart from the others. The girl who, when she has to feed her father's dogs, cringes as she moves toward them, fears their barks and growls. Why does she *have* to feed the dogs?

Her strict father, she told me, *made* her do it.

I, too, fear large, barking dogs.

The scene changes to my mother studying languages and literature in college, to her flapper figure, engaging the interest of men. During this period, she is maid of honor in May 1926, for

142

Major General Thomas P. Lamkin, Commander of the Alabama Division at the 31st Annual Sons of Confederacy Veterans. She wears a circular gold badge with an imprint of soldiers on horses, a red satin ribbon attached, and the nameplate of "Maid of Honor." In her "My Memory Book" from the 1920s, she places her badge next to a sepia photo of Lamkin in uniform, holding himself erect with the pride of his rank in the "War of the South." On the lower part of the page is a letter of June 7, 1926, from Lamkin to Miss Nannie B. Chandler, "My dear little maid," thanking her for a letter she must have written to him after the convention.

Now I see her playing the piano for the Baptist Howard College Men's Glee Club and the College Girl's Glee Club, where she also sang first soprano. In one scene, the keyboard has somehow collapsed into her lap. My mother does not pause. She finishes the program.

In another scene, I envision her dancing the Charleston, moving across the floor with her hands crossing over each other and touching her knees, or the Black Bottom, a couple's dance which hit its peak in 1927, the year she graduated from college and took her first job.

I see her next, this college graduate, teaching high school English and languages in the town only ten miles away from her hometown of Decatur. She is a popular teacher despite the "eyes in the back of her head" that her students swears she has. She sings with the high school chorus, coaches girls' athletics (an unlikely role for her), and is a language and English teacher. But only for one year.

Her marriage to Woodford Owen Nelson in March 1928 takes her out of her teaching job and places her at home for the rest of her life. My father's work for the IRS takes them to Birmingham, Athens, Mobile, Sheffield, and Florence, Alabama. This begins the life-long process of movement. She has two daughters in the early 1930s, both born at home in Athens, Alabama. Her husband's enlistment in World War II sets her on a path of constant change and adjustment, all of which she manages, and manages well.

She moves when the Army tells her to move. Sometimes she must stay when he leaves. On one occasion during World War II, she watches her husband board a train, headed for an overseas assignment in New Guinea. And as she told me many times, after the train leaves the station, she faints and crumples to the ground, as if she has held in her fear and sorrow at his leaving so that he will not see her.

Her husband returns from New Guinea, the war ends and he stays in the Army, and now in middle age, my mother becomes pregnant with her third daughter. In the early years of this child's life, her husband teaches ROTC at Purdue University. His drinking reaches a crisis level. Her older daughters beg her to leave him. Her response is, "I'm married for life."

She follows her husband to Fairbanks, Alaska, Ladd Air Force Base, taking her middle and youngest daughters. The oldest has left home, married, and had a child. Nannie B. lives through the glare of unending Alaska summer and the endless blackness of winter days where light appears in the sky only when it's cloudless enough for her to see the stars or the Northern lights stream above her. In winter, she waits for her youngest daughter's school bus as it arrives in the darkness. She and her daughters, and sometimes her husband, walk through dark underground tunnels to shop and see movies. Here at Ladd Air Force Base, a strategic base during the Cold War, she is only a short plane ride from the Soviet Union. During the daytime, soldiers practice maneuvers outside her ground-floor windows, clutching rifles and hiding behind birch trees. In the middle of the night, a siren blasts through the quiet. Her husband rises from their bed and dresses. He leaves and he tells her that he does not know when, or if, he will return. She tells this to her youngest daughter, now five years old.

But her husband does return every time. The family transfers back to the continental United States, first to Texas, then to Oklahoma, and throughout these years, she helps her youngest child face the challenges of leaving friends and schools.

In Oklahoma, she sees her husband, whose first love is the Army, humiliated by a loss of rank from lieutenant colonel to master sergeant, either due to a bureaucratic oversight or his indiscretion with drink. She will never know the truth. When her husband leaves

144

for Korea and an eighteen-month stint with the Corps of Engineers as an enlisted man, she moves with her daughters to Houston. When her husband returns, she watches him sit in a chair, a beer and a lit Chesterfield cigarette in hand, as he stares at a black-and-white television until he falls asleep, the test pattern etching shadows and glimmers of light on his face.

For the next assignment of four months, she lives with her husband and youngest daughter on a remote Army base in the hills of Missouri. Her middle daughter has left home to find her own way. My mother tries to plant petunias in the nutrient-poor soil by her little "cracker box house" in the neighborhood where enlisted soldiers live. The petunias die and the base is hit by a tornado. In the fall of 1958, she makes her last Army move with her husband and daughter to the Upper Peninsula of Michigan. Again she makes a major transition, this one from the steamy heat of Missouri to the severe cold, finding her way, as always, to new friends, writing her poems, watching her last daughter grow into puberty. In the middle of this chapter of her life, she and her daughter leave husband and father to travel the length of the country on a bus when her middle daughter Marjorie becomes ill. Neither she nor the family will know that the illness is multiple sclerosis, waiting to emerge in just a few years. For three months, she helps her youngest daughter struggle (again) with changing schools and expectations, not to mention family tensions that arise from three families—Marge and her husband, Betty and her husband and son, and Bee and her daughter, living in one small, three-bedroom house. She lives through disruptions and shouting, moves to another apartment and finally three months later, she gratefully returns with her youngest daughter to her husband and to the northern Michigan town that she has grown to love.

As always, this does not last. It does not matter whether or not she loves the place. Her husband retires, and she must leave again with him and her daughter to return home to Alabama, to the very town where she taught school for one year. She watches her youngest daughter complete high school and leave for college, marry for the first time. She buries her in-laws, and then she buries her husband. Finally, she buries the stepmother who raised her, Nannie Dixie Robinson Chandler.

For twenty-five years, she remains in this little town, a widow. She tutors and teaches numerous young folks who study poetry, English grammar, Latin, and French. And she never takes a dime from any of them.

In her last years, when her memory and balance are slipping away, she moves one more time, back to Michigan to be near her youngest, who teaches college and wants her mother nearby. This third daughter will finally meet the partner she will have for the rest of her life, and Nannie B. will see that all is well.

In her ninety-sixth year, when her youngest is at a conference, she realizes that she is dying. In the hospital, her grandson, who carries the name of her husband, strokes the back of her head and tells her, "Wait for Mom, Mama Bee. She'll be here soon." She waits, and when her daughter arrives, she asks, "How was your trip, Nancy?" She quips that she could use a gin and tonic. Then through the next hours, she gasps for breath. She will say over and over again, "I want to go to bed, up there." Between gasps, she tells her daughter, "Let me go. Let me go." Her daughter releases her. "You've lived a long and good life, Mom. You deserve to rest."

She nods her head. She understands that she is being released. Her gasps become quicker, as if she is delivering a child, as her mother delivered her some ninety-six years ago. She gasps once more, and then she is gone.

Nancy Owen Nelson

CHAPTER NINETEEN
Epitaph

I DO NOT BELIEVE my grandfather Robert Edward Chandler was an evil man. I see him as a man heartbroken by his young wife's death, unable to do more than give grim orders to a stonemason to put up a rude stone with his wife's name misspelled, without dates, with only "wife of," and not "beloved." That is all he could do for her and for himself.

For his baby girl he found a woman, his wife's sister, Mary, who would take her newborn niece into her home and raise her as her own child. Mary already had four daughters and a six-year-old son, John. Robert's little girl, Nannie B., would live in this home for three years until he took her home with a new wife.

Robert Chandler meant well, I'm sure. He married another woman, also named Nannie, who was much younger than his first wife. Maybe he hoped that this Nannie would not die on him, that she would be both mother to his first child and to other children who came along.

But he did not make sure the little girl knew about her mother, what she looked like, what she loved, how she sang or played piano, what she wore. There were few photos available in the earlier 1900s, only ones made for formal family portraits such as our photo of the Russell sisters or Robert Chandler with his baby girl. No picture albums for the little girl to look at, no photograph of her mother that she could study, perhaps to stroke her cheek as if she was really touching her. Robert did not make sure that his little girl felt safe to ask about her mother. In fact, as I found out from my Cousin Helen, his new wife was jealous of his first wife. Robert allowed her jealousy to limit the information that my mother received.

I do not understand Robert Chandler's reasons for this absence of information about his first wife. He may have wanted to hide his sadness from little Nannie B. Only when he saw his first wife in his little girl as she played piano could he bring himself to speak of her, and only to the little girl as "your mother." I imagine he could not utter her full name.

No, he was not an evil man. He was a sad man, one who chose a new wife to assuage his pain and bring him other children.

I wonder about his early death of cancer at age fifty-four, when his youngest child, David, was only three years old. Was his early demise due to a life of pushing away the pain and grief of Nannie B. Russell's death?

I will never know. As far as I understand, there are no records from Robert Chandler's life. My mother mentioned a fire in the family home that destroyed most all of the contents. Any letters or journals were probably burned.

What I am left with is remnants of people's stories, historical documents, and a grave in rural Alabama.

When I released my mother, when I lay on the ground next to my grandmother's grave, when I coiled my mother's hair around her mother's buttons, I touched and felt the vibrations of my own history, the blood and bone, the flesh that helped to bring me and my sisters into existence.

This blood and bone, this flesh, is a part of me and will be until the energy that is my soul leaves the matter that is my body. This matter will return to its origin.

I am hundreds of miles away from where my mother and my grandmother are buried. Yet in the long, cosmic view, I am within them and they are within me. We are mingled as soul and energy. We are in one body.

This writing is my gift to Nannie B. Russell Chandler and Nannie B. Chandler Nelson. May they never again be blotted out, erased, or forgotten.

This writing is a gift to me as well.

Dearborn, Michigan
September, 2014.

LETTING GO: A LETTER

July 12, 2014

Dear Mom,

 Today is your 109th birthday. That many years ago, you came out of your mother, who gave you her name. You were together one hour, and then separated for 107 years until I joined your hair with her buttons.

 I thought I had finished with the writing, that I had paid tribute to you, Nannie B. Chandler Nelson, and to your mother, Nannie B. Russell Chandler.

 But not so. I find that the pain and sorrow, the darkness and the leaching out of life that you both experienced is in my body as well. I've inherited it. I must let it go.

 Today is a lunar perigee, which means that today, the moon will be closer to the earth. It will be larger, and it will dominate the sky.

 But there are three super moons this year—today, August 10, and September 9. To me, the three moons represent your mother, you, and me.

 I will celebrate our trio on these three days. Today is your mother's day of celebration because while it is your birthday, it is her day of transition. You thought you never knew her, yet I think you really did know her in striving to know yourself, what part of her you carried in your body, that which wasn't inherited from your father.

 You had her music, her singing voice, her sense, I'm sure, of the rhythms and chords of musical notation, her gift of playing the piano. I imagine also that she gave you her sensibility, her sensitivity to and caring of other people. That's what you always showed in your lifetime. I can imagine that the first Nannie B. was that way.

 You also inherited her trauma. What she must have felt when you were taken from her arms, when she could not live but one hour with her

150

child. Her trauma became yours. And because no one would speak of her, you carried it like a cancer, like an aching wound that had no name.

When you passed, you released the trauma, as your mother did when she breathed her last breath.

Now it is my turn. I will breathe out the original sin that I carried with me from my birth, the sin of guilt and responsibility I never really understood. Until I went to Nannie B. Russell Chandler's grave, I had no real sense that I carried her, and you, in my body.

I release that sin, that angst, that sorrow. I give it to you and your mother because you have released your own long ago. You will release mine. It will go into nothingness. I will not give it to my son or my granddaughter.

But I do not release you. I do not release my grandmother. I keep you both closer in my heart and body than I ever could have while carrying this aching, dark pain. Now you are both blended in me, inseparable. The rest of my life I will nurture those things I've learned from both of you.

With all of my love always, Nancy

---

[i] From *Bethel Primitive Baptist Church: History, 1823 – 1998* by Elder Ricky Siniard.

[ii] Email of January 30, 2012. Sherman Isbell has given written permission to use his emails in this work.

[iii] Email of December 13, 2011.

[iv] Sharon Marcus, *Between Women*, 43.

[v] From *The Samuel Butler Chronicle* by Almira B. Butler. Huntsville: AM Press, 1980.

[vi] Portions of this chapter are published in the *Birmingham Arts Journal, Vol. 10, Issue 3.*

[vii] An audio version of this homily is available on the author's web site.

[viii] Reverend Mohr has given verbal permission to use his comments in this work.

Searching for Nannie B.

ABOUT THE AUTHOR

NANCY OWEN NELSON was raised in a military family who visited their home state of Alabama yearly. Her father retired to Hartselle, Alabama in 1960. She has published articles in several academic journals and anthologies. She is co-editor of *The Selected Letters of Frederick Manfred: 1932-1954* (University of Nebraska Press, 1989) and editor of *Private Voices, Public Lives: Women Speak on the Literary Life* (1995, University of North Texas Press) and *The Lizard Speaks: Essays on the Writings of Frederick Manfred* (the Center for Western Studies, 1998). She has a published poetry in the *What Wildness is This?* (University of Texas Press, March 2007) as well as in the *South Dakota Review* and *Graffiti Rag* and has creative nonfiction pieces in *Mom's Writing Literary Journal* (Fall, 2008), *Lalitamba Journal*, and *Roll* (Telling Our Stories Press, 2013). She is currently teaching writing in several colleges and conducts a memoir workshop for Springfed Arts (a Detroit literary/music organization).

Made in the USA
San Bernardino, CA
04 July 2015